REVIVAL'S GOLDEN KEY

Official Training Manual for End-Time Believers

RAY COMFORT
with KIRK CAMERON

Bridge-Logos *Publishers*

Gainesville, Florida 32614 USA

Revival's Golden Key:
Official Training Manual for End-Time Believers

Bridge-Logos Publishers
P.O. Box 141630
Gainesville, FL 32614, USA
www.bridgelogos.com

ISBN 0-88270-930-5

Edited by Lynn Copeland

Design and production by Genesis Group
(design@genesis-group.net)

Cover by Joe Potter (joepotter.com)

Printed in the United States of America

Second printing, 2003

Woe to you lawyers! For you have taken away the key of knowledge. You did not enter in yourselves, and those who were entering in you hindered.

LUKE 11:52

My special thanks to
Joc & Walter Greeman, Mark Cahill,
Jay & Margie Grosfeld, Larry & Carol Ells,
Jeff & Melissa Loritz, Felicia Woodson,
"Scotty" & Carol Scott, Larry Taggart,
Dan Arnold, Rick Hart, Tammy Hays,
and Ashley and Larry Lee for their
faithful support of our ministry,
and to Lynn Copeland for her
invaluable editorial work.

CONTENTS

FOREWORD

When I came to Christ at the age of 18, I was a successful young actor who had attained riches and fame. But a faithful pastor helped me realize that my wealth and Hollywood charm wouldn't help me one bit on Judgment Day. I learned that because God is holy and just, He couldn't be bribed. Despite the fact that I was admired by my fans and considered to be a good person, I came to understand that I had sinned against God and needed His forgiveness. I learned about God's love and mercy shown through Jesus' death on the cross, and it overwhelmed me. I wholeheartedly turned from my sin, trusted God to forgive me, and asked Him to make me the man He wanted me to be. Someone gave me a Bible which I began to read, and I fell in love with the One who first loved me and gave His own life for me.

Thirteen years later, I can honestly say that nothing in all my life compares with the joy of knowing Jesus Christ as my Savior and Lord. But after learning the principles contained within this book, I fell to my knees with a deeper sense of brokenness and gratitude than ever before. God has used these foundation-shaking principles to open my eyes and change me forever. That is why I wanted to share my thoughts and experiences with you. This teaching has not only changed the way I present the gospel, but it has shattered my lukewarm concern for my unsaved family and friends. If this book has the same effect upon others, we will surely see a revival within our generation.

This book—a devastating blow to Satan's best kept secret —has slipped through the enemy's fingers and landed in your hands. Read with caution. Prepare to be shocked. Its message is powerful and life-changing. Don't let anything distract you as you carefully read this book.

May God bless you with a deeper understanding of His truth and His love, and empower you with His own passion to reach the lost.

KIRK CAMERON

PREFACE

As I waited to take off in a plane in the early 1980s, I noticed that someone had removed a newspaper from the seat pocket in front of me, leaving a small portion of the paper sitting precariously at the top of the seat pocket. I leaned forward, took hold of the two-inch-square piece of paper and mumbled in semi-jest, "Could be a word from the Lord." As I turned it over, my eyes widened as I read, "I have yet many things to say unto you, but ye cannot bear them now (John 16:12)." I remember being mystified by the words "ye cannot bear them now."

One year later I went into the deepest, darkest, most frightening experience of my life. It left me so broken, for over a year I couldn't even muster enough courage to eat a meal with my family. It took five long years to recover from the experience.[1]

I now understand what the word "bear" means. In the original it means to "endure, declare, and receive." That terrible experience left me with a broken spirit. It brought me to a point where I could receive, endure, and declare the many things I had learned. This book is about those "many things."

In October 2001, when Kirk Cameron and I met,[2] one of the first things he said was, "How can we get this teaching out there?" We decided that one way was for him to not only lend his name to this book, but to give his personal comments in the places that stirred his heart. (His comments and additions appear in shaded boxes.)

This is a training manual. Its purpose is simply to equip you to share the gospel biblically. We suspect that after reading it you will want to learn more, so Kirk and I have also worked together on another one of our publications. It is called *The End-Time Believer's Evidence Bible*. This is a munitions resource for the soldier of Christ, and it is designed to help you hone your evangelistic skills to hit your target with precision and power. It was a finalist for the 2002 Gold Medallion Book Award, and it has been commended by Josh McDowell, Franklin Graham, Dr. D. James Kennedy, and many other Christian leaders. Check out the Bible at www.livingwaters.com. While you're there, sign up for the free newsletter, join what we have called "the G-Force," and together let's reach this world for Jesus Christ while there is still time.

PHENOMENAL GROWTH

1

We live in exciting times. All around us we are seeing signs of the end of the age. Nation is rising against nation. There are wars, earthquakes, famines, and violence. The Jews are back in Jerusalem, and the city has become a "burdensome stone" to the nations. Jesus said that iniquity (lawlessness) would abound, and it certainly is. At the same time, we have seen the incredible phenomenon of the rise of megachurches with congregations in the tens of thousands. We have heard of millions coming to the Savior in Russia, China, and Africa. Pockets of revival have sprung up in the United States and different parts of the world. These are exciting times.

With all the excitement, it doesn't seem that many have noticed a few statistical inconsistencies. In 1996, a survey conducted by the Alan Guttmacher Institute in New York found that "eighteen percent of abortion patients describe themselves as born-again or evangelical Christians" (*U.S. News & World Report*, August 19, 1996). That is, of those who murdered their own child, nearly one in five professed faith in Jesus Christ. That is a little difficult to reconcile with the fact that Christians are supposed to love God and to love others as much as they love themselves.

In 1994, the Barna Research Group found further evidence that all is not well in the contemporary Church. A survey revealed that one in four American adults who said they were born-again believe that Jesus "sinned" while He was on the earth. Think for a moment of the implications of such a theology. Here we have millions of "believers" who supposedly confess that Jesus is Lord, and yet they think He sinned. Therefore, they believe the Bible is inaccurate when it says that Jesus "knew no sin" (2 Corinthians 5:21), that He was "in all points tempted as we are, yet without sin" (Hebrews 4:15), and that He "committed no sin, nor was guile found in His mouth" (1 Peter 2:22). This also means Jesus wasn't the "spotless" Lamb of God the Scriptures say He was. His sacrifice wasn't perfect, and when God accepted His death as an atonement for our sins, He sanctioned a "contaminated payment" and is therefore corrupt by nature.

Sadly, these multitudes who profess faith in Jesus are perhaps strangers to true regeneration.

Some years ago, the Barna Research Group revealed that sixty-two percent of Americans claim to have "a relationship with Jesus Christ that is meaningful to them." Yet a Gallup Poll taken around the same time found that, of those Americans who say they have a relationship with the Savior, approximately ten percent were what Gallup called "a breed apart":

> They are more tolerant of people of diverse backgrounds. They are involved in charitable activities. They are involved in practical Christianity. They are absolutely committed to prayer.

That sounds like *normal* biblical Christianity. That means there is a great mass of people who say that Jesus Christ is meaningful to them, but who are not "a breed apart." They are not involved in good works, nor are they tolerant of others. Neither are they involved in practical Christianity nor committed to prayer. That means there are millions of people in America who insinuate that they belong to Jesus Christ, but whose lives don't match their claims. Another Gallup Poll found "very little difference in the behavior of the churched and unchurched on a wide range of items including lying, cheating, and stealing."

One in four American adults who said they were born-again think that Jesus "sinned" while He was on the earth.

We are told that ninety-one percent lie regularly at work or home, eighty-six percent lie regularly to parents, and seventy-five percent lie regularly to friends (*The Day America Told the Truth*). A massive ninety-two percent own a Bible, but only eleven percent read it daily. Surveys also show that ninety percent of Americans pray, but eighty-seven percent do not believe in all of the Ten Commandments. To top it off, according to the Roper Organization, sixty-one percent believe that "premarital sex is not morally wrong."

When I find myself in a hotel, I usually channel-surf in an effort to find something wholesome. This often means crossing the polluted and shark-infested waters of MTV. If anything epitomizes this foul-mouthed, sexually perverted, depraved, blasphemous, and rebellious generation, it is MTV. An article in the December 1995 *Youth Leader* magazine stated:

> More Christian teens watch MTV each week (forty-two percent) than non-Christians (thirty-three percent), according to a Barna Research Group survey of evangelical teens.

The article went on to quote Barna surveys showing that of these same teens, sixty-five percent said they prayed daily. An amazing seventy-two percent believed the Bible. However, over a three-month period, sixty-six percent confessed that they had lied to a parent or teacher, fifty-five percent had had sex, fifty-five percent had cheated on an exam, and twenty percent had either gotten drunk or used illegal drugs.

A Christian youth leader was interviewed recently on a popular national radio program. He spoke with great concern of the fact that young people were "leaving the Church in droves." Then he cited the number-one reason they were turning their backs on God. He had taken a survey to find out why and discovered that it was a "lack of opportunity in the Church," inferring that the Church should get its act together and give young people more opportunity.

Ask any pastor if there is "opportunity" to serve within his church and he will no doubt tell you of the lack of people to teach Sunday school, to visit the sick and the elderly, to go out with the evangelism team, to clean the church building, etc.

The truth is, if someone's heart is still in the world (if he is a "Judas" at heart), he will find *any* excuse to go back there. If Judas had been given a survey form to fill out, he would likely have had many justifications for his betrayal of the Savior and his falling away:

- He was publicly humiliated by Jesus when he suggested giving funds to the poor.

- He felt a deep sense of rejection because he was not part of the "inner circle."

- He needed the money.

- The chief priests made him do it.

- The devil made him do it.

- The responsibility of looking after the finances became too much for him.

- He was abused as a child.

- He had a betrayal syndrome.

- He lacked a father figure.

- He didn't think his actions would have the grisly repercussions they had.

There are some who don't believe that Judas was even a Christian. There is a good reason for this: Jesus said of him, "One of you is a devil." That's not something one would be likely to say about one of God's children.

Judas Iscariot was a hypocrite—a *pretender*. He had no idea who Jesus was. He complained that an act of sacrificial worship was a waste of money. He thought the expensive ointment with which a woman anointed Jesus should have been sold and the money given to the poor. Jesus of Nazareth just wasn't worth such extravagance. In his estimation, He was only worth about thirty pieces of silver.

The Bible tells us that Judas was lying when he said that he cared for the poor. He was actually a thief, who so lacked a healthy fear of God that he was stealing money from the collection bag (John 12:6).

THE PARABOLIC KEY

When Jesus gave His disciples the Parable of the Sower, it seems that they lacked understanding of its meaning: "He said to them, 'Do you not understand this parable? How then will you understand all the parables?'" (Mark 4:13).

15

In other words, the Parable of the Sower is the key to unlocking the mysteries of all the other parables. If any message comes from the parable, it is the fact that when the gospel is preached, there are true and false conversions. This parable speaks of the thorny ground, the stony ground, and the good soil hearer—true and false converts.

Once that premise has been established, then the light of perception begins to dawn on the rest of what Jesus said in parables about the kingdom of God. If one grasps the principle of the true and false being *alongside each other*, then the other parabolic teachings make sense: the Wheat and Tares (true and false), the Good Fish and Bad Fish (true and false), the Wise Virgins and the Foolish (true and false), and the Sheep and Goats (true and false).

After the Wheat and Tares parable, Jesus gave the Parable of the Dragnet:

> "Again, the kingdom of heaven is like a dragnet that was cast into the sea and gathered some of every kind, which, when it was full, they drew to shore; and they sat down and gathered the good into vessels, but threw the bad away. So it will be at the end of the age. The angels will come forth, separate the wicked from among the just, and cast them into the furnace of fire. There will be wailing and gnashing of teeth." Jesus said to them, "Have you understood all these things?" They said to Him, "Yes, Lord" (Matthew 13:47–51).

Notice the good fish and the bad fish were in the net together. The *world* is not caught in the dragnet of the kingdom of heaven; they remain in the world. The "fish" that are caught are those who respond to the gospel—the evangelistic "catch." They remain together until the Day of Judgment.

Judas was a false convert. It would seem that he was a

thorny-ground hearer. The Bible says of the thorny-ground hearer: "The cares of this world, the deceitfulness of riches, and the desires for other things entering in choke the word, and it becomes unfruitful" (Mark 4:19). Some of these professing Christians stay within the Church; others leave it in "droves."

False converts *do* have a measure of spirituality. Judas did. He convinced some of the disciples that he did truly care for the poor. He *seemed* so trustworthy that he was the one who looked after the finances. When Jesus said, "One of you will betray me," the disciples didn't point the finger at the faithful treasurer, but instead suspected themselves, saying, "Is it I, Lord?"

If one grasps the principle of the true and false being alongside each other, then the other parabolic teachings make sense.

That's why it's not surprising that so few within the Body of Christ would ever suspect that we are surrounded by those who fall into the "Judas" category. However, alarm bells should go off when we look at statistics such as those just cited. A warning should sound when it seems that the Church ought to have massive clout in society, but sadly lacks it when push comes to shove. With our millions of professed believers we can't even outlaw the killing of the unborn. Something is *radically* wrong. But before we look at the remedy, we are going to consider the cause.

2

THE WAY OUT
OF PROBLEMS

I n light of alarming statistics, few could deny that the Church as a whole has fallen short of the powerful, disciplined, sanctified Church we see in the Book of Acts. This has happened because the enemy has very subtly taken the focus off our message. Instead of preaching the good news that sinners can be made righteous in Christ and escape the wrath to come, the gospel has degenerated into the pretext that we can be made happy in Christ and escape the hassles of this life.*

* Read this sentence again. Make sure you understand the difference. —KC

One of America's largest publishers recently produced a quality, full-color publication that epitomizes the promise of a hassle-free life. Entitled *Is There a Way Out?*, it reads:

> Everyone is looking for a way out of their problems. There's no easy way out. You won't get respect by joining a gang. You won't find love in the back seat of a car. You'll never find success by dropping out of school. And the chances are about one million to one that you'll win the lottery. If you're *really* serious about mak-

ing your life better, then try God's way. God gets right to the source of most of our problems: sin.

It may sound admirable—and even biblical—to imply to sinners that Christianity promises "a way out of their problems," but it's just not true.

It seems that we are so entrenched in traditional evangelism that we don't equate *real* life with the message we preach. It's no exaggeration to say that the following words are commonplace in many pulpits each Sunday morning (I know from many years of itinerant ministry that this is often what happens):

God loves you and has a wonderful plan for your life. He wants to give you *true* happiness and to fill the God-shaped vacuum in your heart that you've been trying to fill with sex, drugs, alcohol, and money. Jesus said, "I have come that you might have life, and have it more abundantly." So come forward now and give your life to Jesus, so that you can experience this wonderful new life in Christ.

While they are coming, let's pray for the Smith family who lost their two children in a car accident this week. Brother Jones has been diagnosed with cancer. Remember to uphold the *whole* family. His wife had another miscarriage on Tuesday, and both of their other children are chronic asthmatics. Sister Bryant fell and broke her hip. She's such a dear saint—she's had trial after trial in her life, especially since the death of her husband, Ernie. Elder Chambers lost his job this week. That will make things difficult for the Chambers family, with his upcoming triple-bypass operation. Sister Lancing died of kidney failure on Monday night. Keep the Lancing family in prayer because it's their third tragedy this year.

How many of you this morning need prayer for sickness or have problems with depression? That many? You had better stay in your seats and we will have a corporate prayer.

Let me tell you about a few of my Christian friends who live in the real world. One went with his wife to a meeting. Their teenage son drove there alone. On the way home, my friend came across an accident, so he stopped to help. When he looked in the vehicle, he saw his beloved teenage son dead—impaled on the steering wheel.

The senior pastor of a church at which I was on staff was once asked to get out of bed at 3:00 a.m. to counsel a man who was waiting in his living room. As he stepped into the room, the man began to cut him up with a machete. The pastor almost died, and was irrevocably scarred both physically and mentally, so that he was unable to minister and required twenty-four-hour care.

We are so entrenched in traditional evangelism that we don't equate real life with the message we preach.

Another pastor friend learned that his wife had multiple sclerosis. Her crippling disease left him as the only one in the family able to take care of their three young boys. Then he was diagnosed with cancer.

One of my graphic artists married a woman whose Christian husband had died of cancer, leaving her to raise five kids. The marriage was fine until she ran off with another man. She left my friend with the one child that was his. Sometime after that, someone broke into his home and beat him to a pulp. He had to be rushed to the hospital for treatment.

One other friend found his beloved wife dead, in utterly tragic circumstances I am not at liberty to print.

On June 19, 2000, five trainees with New Tribes Missions pitched a tent during a violent storm in Mississippi. Jenny Knapp, an attractive twenty-year-old, noticed that rain was causing the roof to cave in, so she lifted the tent pole to raise the height of the roof. Suddenly, a bolt of lightning struck the pole and tore through her body, giving her second-degree burns on her face, arm, and back. Her friends resuscitated her lifeless body and rushed her to the hospital where she was placed in the intensive care unit. The young missionary recovered, but is terribly scarred and partially blind. It is a sad fact of life, but in the real world, lightning falls on the just and the unjust.

At least one church I know of may have noticed the paradox. They were called "The Happy Church," but recently decided, for some reason, to change their name.

I think that if we still want to cling to "God loves you and has a wonderful plan for your life," we had better hide *Foxe's Book of Martyrs* from the eyes of sinners. Speaking of martyrdom, have you ever thought of what it would be like to be huddling together as a family, as hungry and ferocious lions rush into a Roman arena? Have you ever considered what it would be like to be eaten by lions? I have. My fertile imagination runs wild. What do you give the lion to eat first—your arm? How long would you remain conscious as he gnawed on it?

Can you imagine the feelings you would have if you had led your loved ones in a sinner's prayer using the *wonderful plan* hook? Suppose you had read to them from a booklet by one well-known and respected man of God in which he said, "Everyone is seeking happiness. Why, then, are more people not experiencing this happiness? According to the Bible, true happiness can be found only through God's way." What would you tell your beloved family as you look into their terrified eyes? How could you reconcile the word "wonderful" with having the fierce teeth of a lion rip you apart, limb from limb?

These are terrible thoughts, but they are not merely my fantasies. Multitudes of martyrs have suffered unspeakable torture for the name of Jesus Christ. It should not have been a surprise to the early Church when persecution hit them. Jesus warned them that they may have to give their lives for His name's sake. He even said, "Brother will deliver up brother to death, and a father his child; and children will rise up against parents and cause them to be put to death. And you will be hated by all men for My name's sake" (Matthew 10:21,22).

History tells us the fate of the apostles:

- Philip: Crucified, Phrygia, A.D. 54

- Barnabas: Burned to death, Cyprus, A.D. 64

- Peter: Crucified, Rome, A.D. 69

- Paul: Beheaded, Rome, A.D. 66

- Andrew: Crucified, Achaia, A.D. 70

- Matthew: Beheaded, Ethiopia, A.D. 60

- Luke: Hanged, Athens, A.D. 93

- Thomas: Speared to death, Calamina, A.D. 70

- Mark: Dragged to death, Alexandria, A.D. 64

- James (the Less): Clubbed to death, Jerusalem, A.D. 66

Persecution has always been the portion of the godly. According to Scripture, they have been "tortured, . . . had trial of mockings and scourgings, yes, and of chains and imprisonment. They were stoned, they were sawn in two, were tempted, were slain with the sword. They wandered about in sheepskins and goatskins, being destitute, afflicted, tormented—of whom the world was not worthy. They wandered in deserts and mountains, in dens and caves of the earth" (Hebrews 11:35–38).

Perhaps some may argue that the Christian life is a wonderful plan because God works all things out for the good of those who love Him (Romans 8:28). That fact is wonderful in the truest sense of the word. No matter what happens to a Christian, he can rejoice because of that promise.

In 1995, in Mainland China when Li De Xian was arrested for his faith, he no doubt knew that God would work all things together for his good. When he was beaten with a heavy club, kicked in the groin and stomach until he vomited blood, then beaten in the face with his Bible and left bleeding on the floor, the promise remained steadfast.

See if you can find any of the disciples telling sinners that God loved them and had a wonderful plan for their lives.

In 1413, John Huss was summoned to appear before the Roman church council in Constance. When he was thrown into a prison for nineteen months awaiting trial for his faith, he no doubt knew that God would work things out for his good. When he was burned alive at the stake and his charred, lifeless body fell among the ashes, the wonderful promise remained unwavering that God would work such an unspeakable horror out for his good.

According to a Regent University study, in 1998 there were approximately 156,000 Christian martyrs throughout the world. This promise was also true for each and every one of these children of God.

When Muslims burst into churches in Rwanda in the late

1990s and hacked men, women, and children to death with razor-sharp machetes, if the many who bled to death loved God and were called according to His purpose, they too could claim this incredible promise.

If it is wonderful that our Creator does work all things out for good—that He brings good out of every agony suffered by our brethren—why then shouldn't we use that truth as bait when fishing for men? Simply because it's not biblical to do so. Go through the Book of Acts and see if you can find any of the disciples telling sinners that God loved them and had a wonderful plan for their lives. Instead, their hearers were guilty criminals—enemies of God who desperately needed righteousness, not to be told that they could enhance their lives with God's wonderful plan. To a sinner, "wonderful" has *positive* connotations, not *negative* ones of machetes, hatred, persecution, beatings, and martyrdom. If they respond to the gospel message only to improve their lives, when persecution comes, they will be disillusioned and fall away from the faith. This is because many respond experimentally, simply to see if the wonderful life promised by Christians is as good as they make it out to be.

Jesus didn't shield the newly converted Saul of Tarsus from what was in store for him as a Christian. He said, "I will show him *how many things he must suffer* for My name's sake" (Acts 9:16, emphasis added). Stephen was cruelly stoned to death for his faith. James was murdered with a sword. John the Baptist also felt the sharp steel of persecution. Down through the ages, Christians have been hated, persecuted, thrown to lions, and, like Huss, even burned at the stake for the sake of the gospel.

In light of Christians being burned to death for their faith in central Africa in February 2000, perhaps the message "God loves you and has a wonderful plan for your life" applies only to the United States. That may have been the case right up until the shooting death of Cassie Bernall on April 20, 1999. Cassie was shot in the head in Littleton, Colorado, when she said, "Yes" to the question, "Do you believe in God?"

If persecution and hardship are the realities of the Christian life, why in the world would *anyone* in his right mind choose to become a Christian? What would bring someone to the Savior if it were not the promise of a wonderful new life in Christ? We will look at this in the next chapter.

At this point, some readers may feel angry. "Why would anyone expose the truth of persecution for following Jesus? If we do that, we'll scare away the lost and they won't want to become Christians." If this is what you feel, don't stop now. Press on and read the next few chapters. Your anger will turn to joy! —KC

A Lifestyle
Without a Life

T here is perhaps a rational answer to the question, "Does Jesus really solve sinners' problems?" If those who say that "Jesus solves problems" were "converted" under the same gospel they propagate, and did not repent themselves, then there may be some truth in what they are saying. If they continue to live in lawlessness, then they don't have a struggle with the world, the flesh, and the devil. They are friends with the world. They flow with it rather than against it, and therefore don't have "tribulation" in it. Because they don't "live godly in Christ Jesus," they don't "suffer persecution" (2 Timothy 3:12). They are not hated for His name's sake because their lives are no different from those who are in the world. They live in the flesh, and therefore don't struggle to deny the flesh.

Neither do they wrestle against the devil. In fact, he will be pleased with what he sees. They have "found religion," and think that by going to church on Sunday morning they are now all right with God, assuaging their nagging consciences. They joined the fellowship of the church; they enjoy the music, the social activities, the friendship, and the many other benefits of modern Christianity, including what they think is assurance of everlasting life.

They *have* found happiness in their new lifestyle—but they haven't found new life in Christ.

And here's the double tragedy from such error. When the Church declares the message that "Jesus gives happiness," it restricts its field of evangelistic endeavor to those in society who will be interested: *those who are not happy*—individuals with alcohol, drug, marriage, personal, and financial problems.

These "problem" people don't hear the message of sin, righteousness, and judgment, with the command to repent and flee from the wrath that is to come. Instead they hear that Jesus is the answer to their alcohol, drug, marriage, personal, and financial problems. He is the One who can fill the God-shaped vacuum in their lives. Many therefore come only to have their problems solved. They don't repent of their sin, and so they have a false conversion (Mark 4:16,17). They don't become new creatures in Christ. They do "name the name of Christ," but they don't "depart from iniquity" (2 Timothy 2:19). Rather, they bring their sins *and their problems* into the church. This has the following unfortunate effects:

> The call of the gospel is universal, and not confined to the unhappy, "hurting" world, as it is so often promoted.

1. Wearing out the pastor. Instead of being able to fully give himself to feeding the flock of God in the capacity of a shepherd, he finds himself forever counseling those who are "hearers of the Word only and not doers."

2. Tragically, the "happiness gospel" then has the laborers (who are already few in number) tied up in the function of being counselors and propping people up, when these problem people don't need counsel or prop-up. They need repentance.

After speaking of the many problems plaguing the modern Church, J. I. Packer says these insightful words:

> This is a complex phenomenon, to which many factors have contributed; but, if we go to the root of the matter, we shall find that these perplexities are all ultimately due to our having lost our grip on the biblical gospel. Without realizing it, we have during the past century bartered that gospel for a substitute product which, though it looks similar enough in points of detail, is as a whole a decidedly different thing. Hence our troubles.

In a publication titled *What Do You Want From Life?*, the conclusion is drawn that we all want to be happy. Despite the list of things cited—sex, money, friends, fame, love, and so on—the question is: Can we be *truly* and *continually* happy? The answer is, of course, that knowing Jesus produces "ultra happiness...your happiest moment magnified a million times over."

Not many would see that there is anything wrong with this publication. However, the call of the gospel is universal, and is not confined to the unhappy, "hurting" world, as it is so often promoted. The gospel is a promise of *righteousness*, not a promise of happiness, and it therefore may also be offered to those who are *enjoying* the "pleasures of sin for a season." Before my conversion, I was very happy, content, satisfied, cheerful, thankful, and joyful. I was loving life, and living it to the fullest. *Therefore, I was not a candidate for the modern gospel.* However, when I was confronted by the spirituality of God's Law and understood that "riches do not profit in the day of wrath, but *righteousness* delivers from death" (Proverbs 11:4), I saw my need of the Savior.

Let me repeat: Because of the belief that the chief end of the gospel is man's happiness on earth, rather than his righteousness, many fail to see its God-given intention. They think the gospel is only for those who lack money, those who are brokenhearted by life's difficulties, those who are the problem people in society. The belief is further pervaded through popular worship choruses that have splendid melodies, but carry this message: "Heartaches, broken people, ruined lives is why You died on Calvary." Again, like many others, before I became a Christian my life was not "ruined." At the age of twenty I was a successful businessman, with my own house, beautiful wife, car, money, and the freedom (being self-employed) to enjoy it to the full.

> In Hollywood I work with hundreds of people who are very successful and are having an enormous amount of fun. If ever there were a group of people who need the Lord, this is it. But if we limit the gospel to those who have been broken by life's circumstances, many of my colleagues don't qualify. —KC

Evangelistic outreaches are billed as taking the Good News to "the hurting and the needy." Let me repeat: The gospel is not confined to the "hurting" people with ruined lives and heartaches. Both hurting *and* happy people need to be shown their sinful state before God, so they will seek after the righteousness that is in Christ.

Let me further illustrate this common misunderstanding by quoting from another modern publication (I am in no way questioning the sincerity of the author):

> You will desire to be where the Lord is. And He spends His time with those who hurt. At the beginning of His ministry, Jesus quoted Isaiah to describe the work He was called to do: "The Spirit of the Lord is upon me, because He has anointed me to preach the gospel

to the poor; He has sent me to heal the brokenhearted, to preach deliverance to the captives, and recovery of sight to the blind, to set at liberty them that are oppressed, to preach the acceptable year of the Lord" (Luke 4:18,19)... Thus the more you go after God, the deeper you will move into a world filled with hurting people.

In Luke 4:18,19, Jesus gives us a summation of who the gospel is for:

- The poor

- The brokenhearted

- The captives

- The blind

- The oppressed

A quick study will show that Jesus is not necessarily speaking of those who lack financial resources when He speaks of the *poor*. The word means "meek, humble, lowly" —the "poor in spirit" (Matthew 5:3). These are the blessed ones to whom the kingdom of God belongs. The poor are those who know that they are destitute of righteousness. Bible commentator Matthew Henry said of this verse: "To whom He was to preach: to the poor; to those that were *poor in the world*; to those that were *poor in spirit*, to the meek and humble, and to those that were truly sorrowful for sin" (*Matthew Henry's Commentary*, Zondervan Publishing House, p. 1425).

When Jesus speaks of the *brokenhearted*, He doesn't mean those unhappy people whose hearts are aching because they have been jilted by a sweetheart, but those who, like Peter and Isaiah, are contrite and sorrowing for their sin.

Listen to the respected Bible commentator once again:

"For He was sent to heal the brokenhearted, to give peace to those that were troubled and humbled for sins, and to bring them to rest who were weary and heavy-laden, under the burden of guilt and corruption."

The *captives* are those "taken captive by [the devil] to do his will" (2 Timothy 2:26).

The *blind* are those whom "the god of this age has blinded...[to] the light of the gospel of the glory of Christ" (2 Corinthians 4:4).

The *oppressed* are those who are "oppressed by the devil" (Acts 10:38).

> *Only those who are convinced of the disease of sin will appreciate and appropriate the cure of the gospel.*

The gospel of grace is for the humble, not the proud. God resists the proud, but gives grace to the humble (James 4:6). The Scriptures tell us, "Everyone who is proud in heart is an abomination to the Lord" (Proverbs 16:5). He has put down the mighty from their thrones, and exalted the lowly (Luke 1:52). God looks on the man who is poor and of a contrite spirit, and who trembles at His word (Isaiah 66:2). Only the sick need a physician, and only those who are convinced of the disease of sin will appreciate and appropriate the cure of the gospel.

THE ABUNDANT LIFE

Still, the question may arise, why not use the fact that Jesus said He had come to bring us an abundant life (John 10:10) to draw sinners to the Savior? True, the Christian life is full. Consider the life of Paul. Read 2 Corinthians 11:23–28 and see if you think he was bored while being stoned (once), shipwrecked (three times), beaten (three times), and whipped (five times). His life was full. There were also times he wasn't happy. In fact, at one point he was in such despair that he wanted to die (2 Corinthians 1:8).

The apostle gives the carnal-minded Corinthians a glimpse of the abundant life. He told them that he had been condemned to death. He was hungry and thirsty. He lacked clothing. He was beaten and had nowhere to live. Even with his established ministry, he was forced to work with his hands. He was reviled, persecuted, slandered, and treated as the filth of the world. What a terrible, uninviting path Paul walked down. One would think that he would put up a sign saying "Don't enter here." However, he did the opposite. He told the Corinthians to imitate him (1 Corinthians 4:9–16).

WHERE IS GOD'S LOVE?

How was it, then, that the apostle Paul knew God loved him? As we have seen, he was whipped, beaten, stoned, and so depressed that at one point he wanted to die. He was mocked, hated, shipwrecked, imprisoned for years, and then finally martyred. What did he look to for assurance of God's love for him?

He didn't look at his lifestyle because, to the unlearned eye, it didn't exactly speak of God's caring hand for him. His "abundant" life was certainly full, but it wasn't full of what we think it should have been, if God loved him. Picture Paul, lying half-naked on a cold dungeon floor, chained to hardened Roman guards. Look at his bloody back and his bruised, swollen face. "Paul, you've been beaten again. Where are your friends? Demas and the others have forsaken you. Where is your expensive chariot and your successful building program? Where is the evidence of God's blessing, Paul?" you taunt. "What's that? What did you say? Did I hear you mumble through swollen lips that God loves you?"

Paul slowly lifts his head. His blackened, bruised eyes look deeply into yours. They sparkle as he says two words: "...the cross!" He painfully reaches into his blood-soaked tunic and carefully pulls out a large letter he had been writing in his own hand. His trembling and bloodstained finger points to one sentence in particular. You strain your eyes in the dim light and read, "I have been crucified with Christ; it is no longer I who live, but Christ lives in me; and the life which I now live in the flesh I live by faith in the Son of God, *who loved me and gave Himself for me*" (Galatians 2:20, emphasis added).

That was the source of Paul's joy and thus his strength: "God forbid that I should glory except in the cross" (Galatians 6:14). Those who come through the door of seeking happiness in Christ will think that their happiness is evidence of God's love. They may even think that God has forsaken them when trials come and their happiness leaves. But those who look to the cross as a token of God's love will never doubt His steadfast devotion to them.

If the "abundant" life means something different from a "happy" life, who is going to listen if we are blatantly honest about the trials of living "godly in Christ Jesus" (2 Timothy 3:12)? Certainly not as many as are attracted by the talk of a wonderful plan. What, then, is the answer to this dilemma?

The following chapter liberated me from something that had frustrated me for years. The Bible paints such a different picture of the Christian life than the one we try to paint in our churches today. No one in the Bible ever used the "wonderful plan" hook to attract sinners to Jesus. Instead, they employed what Charles Spurgeon called "our ablest auxiliary"—that is, our most powerful weapon. Read on . . . —KC

THE PURPOSE
OF THE LAW

W ho on earth is going to embrace our message if we
  don't use the promise of an abundant, wonderful
new life in Christ? The answer to our dilemma is simply to
do what Jesus did.[3] It seems that the whole of the contemporary Church is running around with placards, T-shirts,
stickers, books, wristbands, etc., asking the question "What
Would Jesus Do?" They ask this for everything but evangelism. What did Jesus do when He confronted a sinner? He
made the issue one of righteousness rather than happiness.
He used the Ten Commandments to show sinners the righteous standard of God.

   In Mark 10:17, a man came running to Jesus, knelt before Him, and asked how he could obtain everlasting life.
This man came "running." He "knelt" before the Savior. It
would seem that his earnest and humble heart made him a
prime candidate as a potential convert. Yet Jesus didn't give
him the message of God's grace. He didn't even mention
the love of God. Neither did He tell him of an abundant,
wonderful new life. Instead, Jesus used the Law of God to
expose the man's hidden sin. This man was a transgressor
of the First of the Ten Commandments. His money was his
god, and one cannot serve both God and money. Then the

Scriptures reveal that it was *love* that motivated Jesus to speak in this way to this rich young man (Mark 10:21).

Every time we witness to someone, we should examine our motives. Do we love the sinner enough to make sure his conversion is genuine; or do we love the feeling of getting another decision for Jesus—when in truth our zeal without knowledge has just produced another potential Judas?

Why did Jesus take the time to use the Ten Commandments? His method seems a bit archaic compared to the quick and easy modern methods of making instant converts. Dr. Martyn Lloyd-Jones gives us the answer:

> A gospel which merely says "Come to Jesus," and offers Him as a Friend, and offers a marvelous new life, without convincing of sin, is not New Testament evangelism. (The essence of evangelism is to start by preaching the Law; and it is because the Law has not been preached that we have had so much superficial evangelism.) True evangelism...must always start by preaching the Law.

What planet is this guy from? "Evangelism must always start by preaching the Law"? Could that be true? Is it biblical? It's what Jesus did, so keep reading to find out why. —KC

When you use the Law (the Ten Commandments) to show the lost their true state, get ready for them to thank you. For the first time in their lives, they will see the Christian message as an expression of love and concern for their eternal welfare, rather than of merely proselytizing for a better lifestyle while on this earth. They begin to understand why they should be *concerned* about their eternal salvation. The Law shows them that they are condemned by God. It even makes them a little fearful.

Look at how John Wesley reconciles the use of the Law (to produce the fear of God) with love:

> The second use [of the Law] is to bring him unto life, unto Christ that he may live. It is true, in performing both these offices, it acts the part of a severe schoolmaster. *It drives us by force, rather than draws us by love. And yet love is the spring of all.* It is the spirit of love which, by this painful means, tears away our confidence in the flesh, which leaves us no broken reed whereon to trust, and so constrains the sinner, stripped of all to cry out in the bitterness of his soul or groan in the depth of his heart, "I give up every plea beside, Lord, I am damned; but thou hast died" (emphasis added).

Perhaps you are tempted to say that we should *never* condemn sinners. However, Scripture tells us that they are *already* condemned (John 3:18). All the Law does is show them their true state. If you dust a table in your living room

Every time we witness, we should challenge our motives. Do we love the sinner enough to ensure his conversion is genuine?

and think it is dust-free, try pulling back the curtains and letting in the early morning sunlight. You will more than likely see dust still sitting on the table. The sunlight didn't create the dust, *it merely exposed it.* When we take the time to draw back the high and heavy curtains of the Holy of Holies and let the light of God's Law shine upon the sinner's heart, all that happens is that the Law shows him his true state before God. Proverbs 6:23 tells us that "the Commandment is a lamp and the Law is light."

You may be familiar with the idea that we should befriend sinners and address their "felt needs," before speaking to them about salvation. This may take weeks, months, or even years before we talk to them about the subject of sin. This concept exists because the Law hasn't been used to show sin in its true light.

Let's see how this idea would work with a child molester. Take for instance the man who, early in 2002, kidnapped a seven-year-old girl from her Southern California home. She was sexually molested, strangled to death, and then her little body was set on fire and left in the desert. Imagine the following: The judge in the case says, "All the evidence is in. You are guilty. However, I don't want to deal with your guilt at the moment. I want to first address your felt needs. Are you happy? Do you have an emptiness inside?" Such talk would be absurd. Any judge who asked such a thing would be thrown out of the court system. The criminal is there because he has committed a serious offense, and that is the only subject that should be addressed. Justice must be served. The man must be punished for his terrible crime. His felt needs have nothing to do with the issue.

We may not think that sin is terrible, but God certainly does—and the only way to understand it from His perspective it to view it through the eyes of the Law. Sin is so serious in His sight that He calls for the death sentence. Therefore, the issue we should address is the sinner's guilt. You may say, "But we can't convince him of guilt. Only the Holy Spirit can do that!" That's true; all we need to do is shine the light of the Law on the sinner's heart. —KC

It was the wrath of the Law that showed the adulterous woman that she was condemned. She found herself between a rock and a hard place. Without those heavy rocks waiting to pound her sinful flesh, she may have died in her sins and gone to hell. I doubt if she would have fallen at the feet of Jesus without the terror of the Law having driven her there. Thank God that it awakened her and caused her to flee to the Savior.

The sinner thinks that he is rich in virtue, but the Law shows him that he is morally bankrupt.* If he does not declare bankruptcy, the Law will mercilessly call for his last drop of blood.

> * See for yourself whether this is true. Ask any sinner if he considers himself to be a good person. The vast majority will say they are. To really get to the bottom of what sinners think of themselves, ask if they believe that they're morally bankrupt like the Bible says (Romans 3:10–12,23; Jeremiah 17:9). Ninety-nine percent of the people you ask (especially church-goers) will emphatically answer, "No!" —KC

What About Legalism?

One evening when I had taken a team to Santa Monica to preach the gospel open-air, it began raining. It not only rained, but the heavens flashed with lightning. Thunder seemed to shake the earth in an unusually severe thunderstorm for Southern California. As a consolation for our team, we purchased two large pizzas to snack on as we took shelter from the pelting rain under a movie theater veranda.

As most of the thirty-member team munched on pepperoni pizza, I noticed the heartwarming sight of an elderly homeless woman having a fight with a ten-inch piece of cheese. It looked like a stretched rubber band as she pulled at it with what teeth she had left. I smiled at her and asked if she wanted me to get her a pair of scissors. Amid the battle, she was able to return a courteous smile.

After she had downed the large slice of pizza, I offered her another one. Surprisingly, she declined. A few minutes later, however, she was battling a second piece. The scene was truly heartwarming.

Suddenly, the police arrived. The theater manager had called the law and told them he wanted the woman removed. There were thirty of us sheltering from the rain, yet he had sorted out a poor, hungry, homeless woman, and was telling the police to force her to move away! I heard the officers protesting that she was just sheltering from the rain. The manager was adamant: the woman had to move on.

The Law's rightful purpose is simply to act as a mirror to show us that we need cleansing.

At that moment I remembered that my pocket was bulging with a bundle of one-dollar bills. Each Friday night I would pull in a crowd by asking trivia questions and giving dollar bills to those who answered correctly. Once the crowd felt comfortable, I would swing from the natural to the spiritual and preach the gospel. As the police officers reluctantly began to move the old woman on, I stepped forward and grabbed her hand. She flinched and turned her fear-filled eyes toward mine, probably thinking that she was being handcuffed. Then she noticed that I had stuffed a wad of bills in her hand, and in a second her fear changed to joy.

The Bible tells us in 1 Timothy 1:8, "Now we recognize and know that the Law is good if anyone uses it lawfully [for the purpose for which it was designed]" (Amplified). Just as the theater manager had used the law for something for which it was never designed—turning an elderly homeless woman out into the rain—so there are those who would use God's Law for something for which it was never designed.

For what purpose was God's Law designed? The following verse tells us: "The Law is not made for a righteous person, but . . . for sinners" (1 Timothy 1:9,10). It even lists the sinners for us: the disobedient, the ungodly, murderers, fornicators, homosexuals, kidnappers, liars, etc. The Law's main design is not for the saved, but for the unsaved. It was given as a "schoolmaster" to bring us to Christ. It was designed primarily as an evangelistic tool.

It is an *unlawful* use of the Law to seek to use it for "justification." The Scriptures make that very clear: "A man is not justified by the works of the law but by faith in Jesus Christ . . . ; for by the works of the law no flesh shall be justified" (Galatians 2:16). The Law's rightful purpose is simply to act as a mirror to show us that we need cleansing. Those who seek to be justified by the Law are taking the mirror off the wall and trying to wash themselves with it.

Neither should the Law be used to produce something we call "legalism." We are given incredible liberty in Christ (Galatians 5:1), and there are those who would seek to steal that liberty by placing the Law on the backs of Christians. Obviously a Christian refrains from "lawlessness." He doesn't lie, steal, kill, commit adultery, etc. However, his motivation for holy living isn't one of legalism imposed on him by the Law. Why does he refrain from sin—to gain God's favor? No. He already has that in Christ. He lives a life that is pleasing to God *because he wants to do all he can to show God gratitude for the incredible mercy he has received through the gospel.* His motive is love, not legalism. D. L. Moody said, "The Law can only chase a man to Calvary, no further."

Why then would any Christian stray into legalism? Why would he begin telling believers what they can and cannot do in Christ? This happens simply because the Law hasn't been used lawfully in the first place. Let me try to explain. If the spiritual nature of the Law is used in evangelism, it will once and for all rid a new believer of any thought of legalism. The Law reveals to him that there is no way he can please God outside of faith in Jesus. As he stands before the ground-shaking thunder and vivid lightning of Mount Sinai, it dawns on him that a holy Creator sees his wicked thoughts. He cringes as he begins to understand that God sees lust as adultery and hatred as murder. The guilty sinner sees that he is "by nature a child of wrath," and therefore flees to shelter in Christ from the rain of God's indignation. He knows that grace, and grace alone, saves him. Nothing in his hand he brings, simply to the cross he clings.

> The guilty sinner sees that he is "by nature a child of wrath," and therefore flees to shelter in Christ.

The true believer is saved knowing that *nothing* commends him to God. After a lifetime of good works, of reading the Word, of prayer and seeking the lost, he is still saved by grace and grace alone. He is an "unprofitable servant" who merely does what he should.

However, he who makes a commitment to Christ without the Law usually comes because he is seeking true inner peace and lasting fulfillment. He comes to fill a God-shaped vacuum in his life. There is no trembling. There is no fleeing from wrath. There is no fear. To him, God is a benevolent, fatherly figure, not wrath-filled. The Law hasn't stripped him of self-righteousness. He doesn't truly believe that his just reward is eternal damnation. Therefore, even as a professing Christian, he thinks that he is basically a good person.

Because of this, he is the one who is likely to think that he is pleasing God by reading his Bible, praying, fasting, and doing good works. He is the one deceived into thinking that somehow his good works commend him to God, and he is therefore the one who is liable to stray into "touch not, taste not, handle not" (Colossians 2:16–23).

The Law, when used lawfully, liberates the believer from legalism. However, if it is neglected before the cross, those who profess faith in Christ are prone to go astray into legalism and then impose demands on other believers, stealing from them the great liberty we have in Christ. (For an article on freedom from Sabbath-keeping, see *The End-Time Believer's Evidence Bible*.)

Look at the function of the Law from the great classic *Pilgrim's Progress* by John Bunyan:

> "It was he [the Law] who did bind my heavy burden upon me." Faithful agrees: "Aye. Had it not been for him, we had both of us stayed in the City of Destruction."
>
> "Then he did us a favor," answered Christian. [Faithful then shows how the Law alarms us:] "Aye. Albeit, he did it none too gently." Then Christian says, "Well, at least he played the part of a schoolmaster and showed us our need. It was he who drove us to the cross."

There are many wonderful references to the work of the Ten Commandments hidden within the pages of God's Word. We will unveil some of these in the next chapter.

OUR BROKEN BACKBONE

5

There are two reasons why the Church would seem to be full of people whose lives don't live up to what they should. As we have seen, the modern gospel has degenerated into a means of happiness, rather than one of righteousness. Second, we have failed to show the sinner that he is a lawbreaker, that he has violated the Law of a holy God.

When I speak of using the Law in evangelism, I am not speaking of a mere casual reference to it, but as the backbone of the gospel presentation, because its function is to prepare the heart for grace. Martin Luther said of the Law, "In its true and proper work and purpose it humbles a man and prepares him—if he uses the Law correctly—to yearn and seek for grace." The Law is the rod and staff of the shepherd to guide the sheep to himself. It is the net of the fisherman, and the hoe of the farmer. It is the ten golden trumpets that prepare the way for the king. The Law makes the sinner thirst for righteousness, that he might live. Its holy light reveals the dust of sin on the table of the human heart, so that the gospel in the hand of the Spirit can wipe it perfectly clean.

The Law should be esteemed by the Church because of its wonderful preparatory work in preparing a sinner's heart for grace. In Joshua 3:14–17, God opened the Jordan River when the feet of the priests, who were carrying the ark of the covenant, touched its waters. Do you remember what the ark contained? It was the two tablets of God's Law. Do you think that God would have opened the waters for the priests if they had complained that the two stone tablets were too heavy, and tipped them into the dirt to lighten their load? Yet that is what many in the contemporary Church have done. The Law is the embodiment of this gospel we carry, but many have "neglected the weightier matters of the Law" and counted them as worthless. They have emptied the Law out of the ark, stripping the gospel of its power.

J. C. Ryle said of God's Law, "But never, never let us despise it. It is the symptom of an ignorant ministry, and unhealthy state of religion, when the Law is reckoned unimportant. The true Christian delights in God's Law (Romans 7:22)."

The Ten Commandments are like the ten camels that carried Abraham's servant in search of a bride for his only begotten son, Isaac (Genesis 24:10–20). When the servant arrived at the city of Nahor, he had his ten camels kneel down outside the city before the well at the time the women go out to draw water. He prayed that the bride-to-be would be evidenced by the fact that she would have consideration for the camels. When Rebekah saw the camels, she *ran* to the well to get water for them.

God the Father sent His Spirit to search for a bride for His only begotten Son. He has chosen the Ten Commandments to carry this special message from His Lord.

While we may not be able to clearly distinguish the Bride of Christ from the rest of this world, the Holy Spirit knows that the primary reason she draws water from the

Well of Salvation is to satisfy the ten thirsting camels of a holy and just Law. The true convert comes to the Savior simply to satisfy the demands of a holy Law. The espoused virgin has respect for the Commandments of God. She is not a worker of lawlessness. Like Paul, she delights in the Law, and says with the psalmist, "I will run in the way of Your commandments" (Psalm 119:32).

The Law is like Aaron's rod that budded (Numbers 17). It looks like hard and dead wood, but from it issues the life of the gospel. If you are not sure if the use of the Law is right, incorporate it into your tabernacle of witness and see if it buds.

"It is the symptom of an ignorant ministry, and unhealthy state of religion, when the Law is reckoned unimportant."

When fiery serpents were sent among Israel, they caused the Israelites to admit they had sinned. The serpents also caused them to look up to a bronze serpent that Moses had placed on a pole. That was the means of their salvation. Those who had been bitten and were doomed to die could look at the bronze serpent and live (Numbers 21:6–9). In John 3:14, Jesus specifically cited this Old Testament passage in reference to salvation from sin. The Ten Commandments are like ten biting serpents that carry with them the venomous curse of the Law. It drives sinners to look to the One lifted up on a cross. It was the Law of Moses that put Jesus on the cross. The Messiah became a curse for us, and redeemed us from the curse of the Law.

The Old Testament said of the Messiah that He would "magnify the Law, and make it honorable" (Isaiah 42:21, KJV). The religious leaders had dishonored the Law, twisting it so that it was of no effect. By their tradition, they had rendered God's Law ineffectual (Matthew 15:6). They even hindered others from entering God's kingdom. This is what Jesus said to them: "Woe to you lawyers! For you have taken away the key of knowledge. You did not enter in yourselves, and those who were entering in you hindered" (Luke 11:52).

The lawyers were professing experts in God's Law. But because they didn't use the "key of knowledge" to bring sinners to the Savior, they hindered its work.

DISCERNING THE DIFFERENCE

God's Law prepares the heart of the sinner for the good news of the gospel. Without this preparatory work, his heart is hardened and he therefore becomes a candidate for a false conversion. Now and then we can catch a glimpse of the difference between the true and false converts. In 1 Kings 3:16–28 we read the famous narrative of two women, both claiming to be the mother of one child. Solomon, in his wisdom, commanded that the baby be cut in half and thus revealed the true mother.

Both of these women dwelt in the same house. The true and false converts dwell together in the house of the Lord. Each of them called Solomon "lord." Both the true and false convert call Jesus "Lord," and it therefore takes the wisdom of Solomon to discern between the true and false convert. What was it that showed Solomon the real mother? It was that the true mother revealed true love. She would rather lose her child than see him cut in two with a sword.

Here is how to tell the true convert from the false. The spurious convert will reveal himself by dividing the Body of Christ in two with some pet doctrine, rather than backing down in humility. He will cut a body of believers in half because of a particular interpretation of Scripture. He lacks the wisdom that is peaceable and open to reason. In contrast, the true convert will strive to keep the unity of the body. He will not even put meat to his mouth if it causes his brother to stumble, let alone push a personal interpretation and cause division.

More often than not, though, the false convert isn't clearly evident. Like the twins in the womb of Tamar, one has a scarlet thread bound around his hand (Genesis 38:27,28). We may not be able to see who has the scarlet thread of the Blood of Christ bound around his hand, but God can. He knows those who are His. It is the Blood that separates the true from the false.

There are, however, many people who seem to stand as testimonies of modern preaching. They more than likely came into the Church under the message of those who do not use the Law as a schoolmaster to bring sinners to Christ. All that these people heard was that Jesus died on the cross for their sins, and that they would never find true peace until they found peace with God. They were told that they needed to trust Jesus Christ. If you are wondering how to reconcile this teaching with that fact, stay with me for the next chapter.

Without this preparatory work, the sinner's heart is hardened and he therefore becomes a candidate for a false conversion.

6

THE KEY WAS IN
THE FOLDING

During a great war, there was a man who invented a parachute that was one hundred percent trustworthy. It made no difference whether the user was large or small; it opened *every* time and got him safely to the ground. The key was in the way it was folded. Every part of the parachute had to be carefully and painstakingly placed in certain positions, following the instructions given by the manufacturer. True, it was somewhat arduous, but it was well worth the effort. It had the effect of ensuring that the life of every precious human being who trusted the parachute would be preserved.

Many years after the war began, a group of young men known as "fast-folders" entered the packing room. These men so influenced the workers with their new fast and easy method of folding that soon they all completely ignored the instruction book given by the manufacturer. Production increased greatly and everyone rejoiced that so much time and effort had been saved.

However, as time passed it slowly became evident that something was radically wrong. In fact, a small group of investigators who went to where the parachutes were being used found to their horror that *of every ten who jumped using the new method, nine tragically fell to their deaths!*

The horrible sight of so many torn and mangled bodies strewn all over the ground sickened them. These weren't just faceless customers. These were husbands, wives, fathers, mothers, sons, and daughters—cherished human beings who plunged to a needless and terrifying death.

A report was quickly relayed to the fast-folders. Many were heartbroken, and immediately went back to the instruction book and corrected their mistake. With great sobriety and care, they began painstakingly folding each parachute exactly as the book instructed. Their knowledge of the tragedies motivated them to make sure that they did their job with uncompromising conviction.

Never once did the Son of God give the Good News to the proud, the arrogant, or the self-righteous.

Yet, there was resistance from a few. Even though they knew that so many lives were being lost, they still refused to follow the instruction book. Unbelievably, they ignored the mass of mangled bodies for which they were directly responsible. *Instead, they pointed to those who had survived their fast-folding method as justification for their technique.*

Likewise, those who preach grace, without first preaching Law to prepare the heart, point to the many thousands remaining in fellowship as evidence to justify the presentation of a gospel that makes no reference to the Moral Standard.

FREE FROM THEIR BLOOD

Since the Fall of man, there has been a great battle for the souls of men and women. Those who have gone before us in past centuries have not had an easy task. Labor in the gospel was often slow and arduous. But they knew if they followed *according to the pattern of God's Word*, with His help, they would eventually deliver sinners from death and hell. If they sowed in tears, they would reap in joy. They wanted, above all things, to be "true and faithful witnesses." If they preached the whole counsel of God, they would be free from the blood of all men. These ministries, of men such as Wesley, Wycliff, Whitefield, Spurgeon, and many others, were greatly effective in reaching the lost. *The key was in the careful and thorough use of the Law to prepare the way for the gospel.*

As time went by, certain men discovered that the message of the gospel could be condensed and presented in a much faster and easier way. Unfortunately, this quick and easy method had a number of problems.

First, its presentation was unbiblical. It didn't follow the scriptural example of presenting the balance of Law and grace, as Jesus did. He always preached Law to the proud and arrogant, and grace to the meek and the humble (Luke 10:25,26; 18:18–20; John 3:1–17). Never once did the Son of God give the Good News (the cross, grace, and mercy) to the proud, the arrogant, or the self-righteous. He followed His Father's example: He resists the proud and gives grace to the humble (James 4:6). Paul did the same, as seen at Athens when he used the essence of the First and Second Commandments to reprove their idolatry, and on other occasions (Romans 2:22). Biblical evangelism is always Law to the proud and grace to the humble. With the Law, we should break the hard heart, and with the gospel, heal the broken heart. Martin Luther, commenting on the right use of the Law, said, "Wherefore this is the proper and absolute use of the Law, by lightning, by tempest and by the sound of the trumpet (as in Mount Sinai) to terrify, and by thundering to beat down and rend in pieces that beast which is called the opinion of righteousness."

Without the Law, there can be no knowledge of sin: "What shall we say then? Is the law sin? Certainly not! On the contrary, *I would not have known sin except through the Law* . . . For apart from the law sin was dead. I was alive once without the Law, but when the commandment came, sin revived and I died" (Romans 7:7–9, emphasis added).

The Law was the instrument of the death of the old nature. It made sure that sinners were truly born again, that the Adamic nature was dealt with by nailing it to the cross. It made certain that the convert was a new creature in Christ.

According to Romans 7:7, the Law of God—specifically the Ten Commandments—is the biblical means of awakening sinners. John Wesley said, "The very first end of the Law [is], namely, convicting men of sin; awakening those who are still asleep on the brink of hell . . . The ordinary method of God is to convict sinners by the Law, and that only. The gospel is not the means which God hath ordained, or which our Lord Himself used, for this end."

A. W. Pink said,

> The unsaved are in no condition today for the gospel till the Law be applied to their hearts, for "by the Law is the knowledge of sin." It is a waste of time to sow seed on ground which has never been ploughed or spaded! To present the vicarious sacrifice of Christ to those whose dominant passion is to take fill of sin is to give that which is holy to the dogs.

Charles Spurgeon, in speaking of preparing the soil of the heart with the plow of the Law, stated:

> One other reason why this soil was so uncongenial

was that it was totally unprepared for the seed. There had been no plowing before the seed was sown, and no harrowing afterwards. He that sows without a plow may reap without a sickle. He who preaches the gospel without preaching the Law may hold all the results of it in his hand, and there will be little for him to hold.

Robbie Flockhart, when he preached in the streets of Edinburgh, used to say, "You must preach the Law, for the gospel is a silken thread, and you cannot get it into the hearts of men unless you have made a way for it with a sharp needle; the sharp needle of the Law will pull the silken thread of the gospel after it." There must be plowing before there is sowing if there is to be reaping after the sowing.

This makes so much sense. I can't believe that I didn't see it before! Because the gospel is all about grace, I had wrongly believed that there was no longer any use for the Law today. But the Law is still the hoe that plows up the soil of the stony heart, and the needle that makes a way for the thread of the gospel. Without the hoe, the soil is not prepared and the seed cannot take root. Without the needle, the thread cannot penetrate. —KC

To what was Jesus referring when He said not to give what is holy to the dogs? To what was He pointing when He said not to cast pearls before swine, lest they trample them under their feet, and turn and tear you in pieces (Matthew 7:6)? The most precious pearl the Church has is "Christ crucified." Preach grace to the proud and watch what they do with it. They will trample the blood of the Savior under their feet with their false profession, and, what's more, they will become enemies of the gospel. If not physically, you can be sure they will tear you in pieces verbally. They have "insulted the Spirit of grace" (Hebrews 10:29). That means they insult the Holy Spirit. "Bitterness" and "backslider" are bad bedfellows for the Church. The proselyte becomes a twofold child of hell.

Those who make a profession of faith without having a humble heart (which the Law produces) have the experience described in 2 Peter 2:22: "According to the true proverb: 'A dog returns to his own vomit,' and 'a sow, having washed, to her wallowing in the mire.'" This is the tragic result of casting pearls of the gospel of grace to the proud, or what the Bible calls "dogs" and "swine."

The Bible presents the great and terrible Day of the Lord as the very reason to repent and trust the Savior.

The false convert has never "crucified the flesh with its passions and desires" (Galatians 5:24). He, like the pig, must go back to wallowing in the mire. Pigs *need* to wallow in mire because they crave the slime to cool their flesh. So it is with the false convert. He never repented, so his flesh is not dead with Christ. It is instead burning with unlawful desire. The heat of lust is too much for his sinful heart; he must go back to the filth.

Yet, the new and modern method of evangelism forsook the Law in its power to humble the proud heart and convert the soul. It did, however, speed the process of evangelism, making it much easier to get "commitments." Also, it stirred less opposition and it seemed to get results. So everyone rejoiced.

Second, modern evangelism failed to mention the fact of Judgment Day. The Bible presents the great and terrible Day of the Lord as *the very reason* to repent and trust the Savior: "Truly, these times of ignorance God overlooked, but now commands all men everywhere to repent, *because He has*

*appointed a day on which He will judge the world in righteous-
ness"* (Acts 17:31, emphasis added). The new presentation
was not faithful to God—it didn't even hint of Judgment
Day's approach. The reason Jesus died on the cross was to
save us from the wrath to come (1 Thessalonians 1:10).
That is the essence of the message of the gospel, but there
wasn't even a mention of hell's existence. The "fast-folders" ripped the heart out of the body of the gospel. General
William Booth, founder of the Salvation Army, warned
that in the twentieth century a gospel would be preached
which promised heaven without mentioning hell. Modern
evangelism did just that. Take the time to study closely the
contents of today's popular tracts and see the flaws of the
fast-folding presentation:

1. No mention of Judgment Day.

2. Not a hint of hell.

3. No use of the Law of God to bring the knowledge of
   personal sin.

4. The gospel is held up as a means of happiness, rather
   than a means of righteousness.

That is a perfect recipe for a false conversion—a stony-
ground hearer. He receives the Word with joy and gladness,
but in a time of tribulation, temptation, or persecution, falls
away. He is like the "young man" in Mark 14:51,52, who
had a "linen cloth thrown around his naked body." When
persecution came, he cast off his covering of righteousness
and fled naked.

False converts are nothing new. George Whitefield said
of his day, "That is the reason we have so many 'mushroom'
converts, because their stony ground is not plowed up; they

have not got a conviction of the Law; they are stony-ground hearers."

A great preacher once said, "Evermore the Law *must* prepare the way for the gospel. To overlook this in instructing souls is almost certain to result in false hope, the introduction of a false standard of Christian experience, and to fill the Church with false converts...Time will make this plain."

God knows that I hesitate to be critical of the authors of modern evangelistic literature. They are sincere, earnest, loving, godly brethren, but their zeal for the lost has lacked knowledge of the use of God's Law, and the results are a devastation that cannot be ignored.

After discovering the rampant hypocrisy among professing believers, Dr. Bill Bright, founder of Campus Crusade for Christ, wrote, "A belief that Christians are entitled to the 'good life' can result in demoralized church members. Expecting the Christian life to be a bed of roses can be very discouraging to a new Christian—and to more mature ones as well—when they are jostled by the storms of life" (*Red Sky in the Morning*, NewLife Publications, p. 218).

In the same book, this godly author weeps at the evident sin in the contemporary Church. Sadly, the horse of holiness has bolted, simply because the gate of the Law has been removed.

Third, the modern method also glossed over sin. Probably the mainstay of the mention of sin in modern evangelism is Romans 3:23: "For all have sinned and fall short of the glory of God." On looking at that Scripture, the question I would ask if I were not a Christian is, "What is meant by 'glory'?" Often we hear how the word "sin" was shouted during archery, to let the archer know that the arrow had fallen short of the target. If I have fallen short of a mark, I would at least want to know what and where the target is *to measure how much I have fallen short*, to know whether I should give up or try another shot.

The Greek word used in that verse is *doxa*, which literally means "honor, worship, praise." Humanity has fallen short by failing to give our Creator the honor, the worship, and the praise due to Him. We have failed to love God with all of our heart, mind, soul, and strength, which is the essence of the Law (Mark 12:30). In fact, "all have sinned" comes in the context of Paul saying that the Law has left the whole world guilty before God (Romans 3:19). By calling "sin!" to a sinner, but failing to tell him anything about the mark for which he is aiming, is to let him think that he can still give it his best shot. However, to display the Law in front of him is to leave him without hope of ever coming near the mark, so that his only hope will be in the Savior.

CHECK THE SOIL

Here is our problem: Up to ninety percent of the evangelistic crop is failing. They wither and die as soon as the sunlight of tribulation, persecution, and temptation shines on them. We encourage them to be watered by the Word. We give them the "fertilizer" of counsel and support. We follow them up thoroughly, but all to no avail.

So, we then need to check the soil. If, before we plant the seed of the gospel, we take the time to thoroughly turn the soil of the heart with the Law, the effect will be the removal of the stones of sin upon repentance.

God has given us insight into the area in which we are planting. The ground of the human heart is very hard. The Scriptures call it a "heart of stone" (Ezekiel 36:26).

I have heard a number of well-known preachers say that it is biblical normality to have seventy-five percent of those coming to Christ fall away. During an altar call,[4] they know that only one in four of those responding to their message will continue in their faith. So, more than likely they are not too alarmed by modern statistics that reveal an eighty- to ninety-percent failure. This thought is based on the Parable of the Sower, which shows that only twenty-five percent of the crop was on good soil (Mark 4:1–20). But I don't think Jesus gave us this parable as a consolation for disappointing evangelistic results. I think He gave it for our instruction.

When we study the parable closely, we see that the good-soil hearer, the *genuine* convert, had some things the other hearers didn't have. He had *understanding* (Matthew 13:23), and he had a *noble and good heart* (Luke 8:15). Does that mean that throughout humanity, there are those who somehow have understanding and a noble and good heart, and we have to keep on sowing until we find them? No, Scripture makes it clear that there is *none* who understands (Romans 3:11), and that the heart of man is not good, but deceitful and desperately wicked (Jeremiah 17:9).

> *Up to ninety percent of the evangelistic crop is failing . . . so we need to check the soil.*

How then did the genuine convert obtain these necessary virtues? It is clear that something from *outside* his own heart must have given him understanding and brought him to a point of having a noble and good heart. The schoolmaster taught him that his heart was wicked. The Law turned the soil of his heart and exposed the stones of sin. When these were removed through repentance, it left the good soil of understanding and a heart that saw itself in truth.

An old movie showed an officer of the law entering an illegal gambling casino. Look at what the manager asked the lawman: "Are you going to speak to the people *before* you arrest them? They *must* have the law spelled out to them so they will know that what they are doing is wrong." Doesn't that make sense? How on earth are the gamblers going to come peacefully if they don't realize they have broken the law?

Using the fast-folding method of modern evangelism, we will continue to produce stony-ground "converts," with the devastating results revealed in the next chapter.

MANGLED BODIES

7

C ome with me now and see a tragic and sobering sight. We will go to the landing ground on which so many have fallen after putting on the Lord Jesus Christ using the fast-folding method.

> Please make sure you don't skip these pages or read them lightly. Go through them thoughtfully and reflectively, as you would walk through a holocaust museum. These statistics are a testimony to an unspeakable human tragedy, affecting not just the body but the soul. —KC

- In a 1990 crusade in the U.S., 600 decisions were obtained. No doubt there was much rejoicing. However, ninety days later, follow-up workers *couldn't find even one* who was continuing in his or her faith. That crusade created 600 "backsliders," or to be more scriptural, "false converts."

- In Cleveland, Ohio, in an "Inner City Outreach," rejoicing no doubt tapered when those who were involved in follow-up once again couldn't find one of the 400 who had made a decision.

- In 1985, a four-day crusade obtained 217 decisions, but according to a member of the organizing committee, ninety-two percent fell away.

- Charles E. Hackett, the Division of Home Missions National Director for the Assemblies of God in the U.S., said, "A soul at the altar does not generate much excitement in some circles because we realize approximately ninety-five out of every hundred will not become integrated into the church. In fact, most of them will not return for a second visit."

- In his book *Today's Evangelism*, Ernest C. Reisinger said of one outreach, "It lasted eight days, and there were sixty-eight supposed conversions." A month later, not one of the "converts" could be found.

- In 1991, organizers of a Salt Lake City concert encouraged follow-up. They said, "Less than five percent of those who respond to an altar call during a public crusade...are living a Christian life one year later." In other words, *more than ninety-five percent* proved to be false converts.

- A pastor in Boulder, Colorado, sent a team to Russia in 1991 and obtained 2,500 decisions. The next year, they found only 30 going on in their faith. That's a retention rate of a little more than one percent.

- In Leeds, England, a visiting U.S. speaker acquired 400 decisions for a local church. Six weeks later only two were going on, and they eventually fell away.

- In November 1970, a number of churches combined for a convention in Fort Worth, Texas, and secured 30,000 decisions. Six months later, the follow-up committee could find only 30 going on in their faith.

- A mass crusade reported 18,000 decisions, yet according to *Church Growth* magazine, ninety-four percent failed to become incorporated into a local church.

- In Sacramento, California, a combined crusade yielded over 2,000 commitments. One church followed up 52 of those decisions and couldn't find one conversion.

- A leading U.S. denomination published that during 1995 they secured 384,057 decisions, but retained only 22,983 in fellowship. They couldn't account for 361,074 supposed conversions. That's a ninety-four percent fall-away rate.

- In Omaha, Nebraska, a pastor of a large church said he was involved with a crusade where 1,300 decisions were made, and not even one "convert" continued in his or her faith.

- Pastor Dennis Grenell from Auckland, New Zealand, who has traveled to India every year since 1980, reported that he saw 80,000 decision cards stacked in a hut in the city of Rajamundry, the "results" of past evangelistic crusades. But he maintained that one would be fortunate to find even 80 Christians in the entire city.

- In the March/April 1993 *American Horizon*, the National Director of Home Missions of a major U.S. denomination disclosed the fact that in 1991, 11,500 churches had obtained 294,784 decisions for Christ. Unfortunately, they could find only 14,337 in fellowship. That means that (no doubt despite the usual intense follow-up) they couldn't account for approximately 280,000 of their decisions.

- A major Christian television network broadcast an interview with a Russian Christian leader on July 5, 1996. She said of Russian converts, "Many thousands have received salvation and healing...but because of there not being many leaders, not many stayed with their faith."

Notice where the blame is laid with the Russian professions of faith. They fell away because they needed more leaders. In light of the fact that God "is able to keep you from falling, and to present you faultless before the presence of His glory with exceeding joy" (Jude 24, KJV), either He wasn't able to keep them, or His hand wasn't in their profession of faith in the first place.

These statistics of an eighty-four to ninety-seven percent fall-away rate are not confined to crusades.

Statistics such as the preceding are very hard to find. What organizing committee is going to shout from the housetops that after a mass of pre-crusade prayer, hundreds of thousands of dollars of expenditure, the use of a big-name evangelist, and truckloads of follow-up, initial wonderful results have all but disappeared? Not only would such news be utterly disheartening for all who put so much time and effort into the crusade, *but the committee has no reasonable explanation as to why the massive catch has disappeared.* The statistics are therefore swept under the hushed carpet of discretion.

A Southern California newspaper bravely printed the following article in July 1993:

"Crusades don't do as much for nonbelievers as some might think," said Peter Wagner, professor of church growth at Fuller Theological Seminary in Pasadena. Three percent to sixteen percent of those who make decisions at crusades end up responsible members of a church, he said. "That's not counting Christians who recommit their lives."

In October 2002, Pastor Ted Haggard of New Life Church in Colorado Springs had a similar finding: "Only three to six percent of those who respond in a crusade end up in a local church—that's a problem...I was recently in a city that had a large crusade eighteen months earlier, and I asked them how many people saved in the crusade ended up in local churches. Not one person who gave his heart to Christ in that crusade ended up in the local church."

These statistics of an eighty-four to ninety-seven percent fall-away rate are not confined to crusades, but are general throughout local church evangelism. In his book *Fresh Wind, Fresh Fire*, Jim Cymbala notes the lack of growth in the Church: "Despite all the Christian broadcasting and high-profile campaigns, the Christian population is not growing in numbers nationally. In fact, church attendance in a given week during 1996 was down to 37 percent of the population, a ten-year low...even though 82 percent of Americans claim to be Christians" (Zondervan, p. 90). The problem is not with the crusades, but with the methods and message of modern evangelism.

Sadly, these are not isolated cases. The mangled bodies of those who are erroneously called "backsliders" lay strewn on the ground as a disastrous result of a fast-folded gospel.

I received the following letter from a pastor in Florida:

> We have seen over a thousand led to the Lord on the streets. Not many of these teens are at church. I've been analyzing this, and last month, for example, I preached face to face on the streets the whole gospel (death, burial, and resurrection) with a focus on repentance and remission to 155 people. Seventy made commitments to

Christ. I know my preaching is correct, but I know I need better follow-up; any recommendations?

His dilemma was that he was preaching the light of the gospel (Christ's death, burial, and resurrection) without using the Law to awaken his hearers. Like many others who see this enigma, he thought that his converts needed more follow-up. A respected minister, whose evangelism program has exploded across the world, said that his policy attempts to get at the heart of the fall-away rate of new converts "by placing great stress on the follow-up." However, to fall into the trap of thinking that follow-up is the answer is like supposing that putting a stillborn child into intensive care will solve the problem.

Author Gordon Miller wrote of his deep concern about the quality of professed converts who stay in the Church, but continue in sin. He said,

> A few months ago, a senior minister of a large growing church rang me about a new situation in their church... An increasing number of converts bring their old ways into their Christian lives and do things that shock their leaders. Here, after further reflection, is an extended version of my response.
>
> The first thing to note is that this church and its ministers haven't diluted the gospel or lowered their standards. The church is one of the best in the country with gifted, godly leaders. They fearlessly preach a no-compromise gospel and are even better at nurture than they were years ago. Yet an increasing number of their numerous converts fail to show evidence of moral change in their lives.

Again, even a "no-compromise gospel" will not awaken sinners. That's not its function.

Perhaps you are thinking, "But I didn't have the Law

preached to me when I came to Christ." Let me ask you a few questions. When you came to the Savior, did you have a knowledge of sin? You must have, or you would not have repented. He who repents turns from sin, and "sin" is transgression of the Law (1 John 3:4).

What then was your sin? Was it lust, adultery, or fornication? If so, then your sin was that you transgressed the 7th Commandment. Did you steal (8th), hate (6th), lie (9th), or blaspheme (3rd)? Were you covetous (10th)? Were you selfish or ungrateful to God? Did you realize that God should be first in your life (1st, 4th)? Or maybe you suddenly discerned that God was nothing like you thought He was (2nd). Did you feel bad about your attitude toward your parents (5th)? How did you know that you had sinned against God? Wasn't it because you knew of the Ten Commandments? Someone, somewhere, somehow had said to you: "You shall not kill, you shall not steal," etc., and your conscience bore witness with the Law. Like Paul, you too can say, "I would not have known sin except through the Law" (Romans 7:7).

IMPERSONAL STATISTICS

On a Saturday sometime in 1998 near Davis, California, a female student from Sacramento and a skydiving instructor (who had made about two thousand jumps) leaped from a plane at ten thousand feet. Both were in their twenties. Tragically, their parachute failed to open and their reserve became tangled in the main chute. Witnesses reported that they heard the young woman screaming for help, *and felt the impact two football fields away*. It was the woman's first jump. Needless to say, it was her and her instructor's last.

I have related this true story to bring a *personal* note to the horror of seeing someone entrust her life to a parachute, and having it fail. One would never forget the sound of a terrified young lady screaming, nor the experience of feeling the earth shake as her fragile body hit the ground. The cold statistic that one in a hundred thousand jumps ends in death somehow loses its reality, but (depending on your tenderness of heart) the details of one young woman's death is heartrending. In the same way, we can speak about how many hundreds of thousands fall away from the faith, and lose sight of the reality that we are speaking about the salvation of *individual* human beings.

I can't put into words the heartbreak of seeing so many spurious converts who have left the Church, and the multitudes of false converts who stay within the Church. A. W. Tozer wrote, "It is my opinion that tens of thousands of people, if not millions, have been brought into some kind of religious experience by accepting Christ, and they have not been saved."

> *We can lose sight of the reality that we are speaking about the salvation of individual human beings.*

We are not talking about mere statistics, but the salvation of men and women from death and eternal damnation in hell. We must put a quick end to the fast and easy method, even though it eliminates the reproach of the gospel and seems to be filling our churches.

Please, don't be tempted to ignore the devastating results of modern evangelism, and to look at those *comparatively* few who are continuing in their faith as justification for the method. Remember, for every 1,000 genuine converts, there are as many as 9,000 who lay mangled on the soil of hard hearts, as a direct result of the quick and easy methods of modern evangelism.

8

MAKING GRACE
AMAZING

An editorial, after reporting that 280,000 converts couldn't be accounted for, concluded by saying, "Something is wrong." It has been wrong for nearly one hundred years of evangelism, since the Church forsook the key to the sinner's heart. As we have seen, when it set aside the Law of God in its function to convert the soul (Psalm 19:7), the Church removed the sinner's means of seeing his need of God's forgiveness.

Romans 5:20 tells us why God's Law entered the scene: "Moreover the law entered that the offense might abound. But where sin abounded, grace abounded much more." When sin abounds, grace abounds "much more"; and according to Scripture, the thing that makes sin abound is the Law.

We can see the work of God's Law illustrated in civil law. Watch what often happens on a freeway when there is no visible sign of the law. See how motorists transgress the speed limit. It would seem that each speeder says to himself that the law has forgotten to patrol his part of the freeway. He is transgressing the law by only 15 mph, and besides, he isn't the only one doing it.

Notice what happens when the law enters the fast lane,

with red lights flashing. The speeder's heart misses a beat. He is no longer secure in the fact that other motorists are also speeding. He knows that he is *personally* as guilty as the next guy, and *he* could be the one the law pulls over. Suddenly, his "mere" 15 mph transgression doesn't seem such a small thing after all; it seems to abound.

Look at the freeway of sin. The whole world naturally goes with the flow. Who hasn't had an "affair" (or desired to) at some time or another? Who in today's society doesn't tell the occasional "white" lie? Who doesn't take something that belongs to someone else, even if it's just "white-collar" crime? They know they are doing wrong, but their security is in the fact that so many others are just as guilty, if not more so. It seems that God has forgotten all about sin and the Ten Commandments—the wicked "has said in his heart, 'God has forgotten; He hides His face; He will never see it'" (Psalm 10:11).

Now watch the Law enter with red lights flashing. The sinner's heart is stopped. He places his hand on his mouth. He examines the speedometer of his conscience. Suddenly, it shows him the measure of his guilt in a new light—the light of the Law. His sense of security in the fact that there are multitudes doing the same thing becomes irrelevant, because every man will give an account of *himself* to God. Sin not only becomes personal, it seems to "abound." His mere lust becomes *adultery of the heart* (Matthew 5:27,28); his white lie, *false witness*; his own way becomes *rebellion*; his hatred, *murder* (1 John 3:15); his "sticky" fingers make him a thief*—"Moreover the law entered that the offense might abound." Without the Law entering, sin is neither personal, nor is it veritable: "For without the Law sin is dead [the sense of it is inactive and a lifeless thing]" (Romans 7:8, Amplified).

* When asked about being a thief, many people will deny stealing *anything*. The label "thief" sounds too harsh for their crimes. But remind them that "stealing" also includes cheating on taxes, neglecting to return library books, taking items from work, "fudging" on an expense report, etc. "Petty" theft is still theft in God's sight. —KC

It was the Commandment that showed Paul sin in its true light, that it is "exceedingly sinful" (Romans 7:13). Paul spoke from his own experience because he sat at the feet of Gamaliel, the great teacher of the Law, and therefore saw sin in its vivid colors.

THE OFFENSE AND THE FOOLISHNESS OF THE CROSS

According to Scripture, "[the real function of] the Law is to make men recognize and be conscious of sin [not mere perception, but an acquaintance with sin which works toward repentance ...]" (Romans 3:20, Amplified).

To illustrate this point, imagine if I said to you, "I have some good news for you. *Someone has just paid a $25,000 speeding fine on your behalf!*" You would probably answer me with some cynicism in your voice, "What are you talking about? I *don't have* a $25,000 speeding fine!" Your reaction would be quite understandable. If you don't know that you have broken the law in the first place, the good news of someone paying a fine for you won't be good news; it will be foolishness to you. My insinuation of unlawful activity will even be offensive to you.

But if I were to put it this way it may make more sense: "Today, the law clocked you traveling at 55 mph in an area designated for a blind children's convention. You totally ignored ten clear warning signs saying that the maximum speed was 15 mph. What you did was extremely dangerous. The fine is $25,000 or imprisonment. The law was about to take its course when someone you don't even know stepped in and paid the fine for you. *You are very fortunate.*"

Can you see that telling you the good news of the fine being paid, without first telling you that you have broken the law, will leave you thinking that the "good news" is nothing but nonsense? However, clearly making known your transgression gives *sense* to the good news. An unclouded explanation of the law, *so that you can plainly see your violation*, helps you understand and appreciate the news that your fine has been paid.

In the same way, telling someone the good news that Jesus died on the cross for his sins makes no sense to him: "For the message of the cross is foolishness to those who are perishing" (1 Corinthians 1:18). Therefore, it is also quite understandable for him to say, "What are you talking about? I haven't got any 'sins.' I try to live a good life," etc. Your insinuation that he is a sinner, when he doesn't think he is, will be offensive to him.

But those who take the time to follow in the footsteps of Jesus and open up the spirituality of the Law, carefully explaining the meaning of the Ten Commandments, will see the sinner become *convicted by the Law as a transgressor* (James 2:9). Once he understands his transgression, the good news will be neither offensive nor foolishness, but the power of God to salvation.

WHAT 'SIN' ARE YOU TALKING ABOUT?

When David sinned with Bathsheba, he broke all of the Ten Commandments. He coveted his neighbor's wife, lived a lie, stole her, committed adultery, murdered her husband, dishonored his parents, and thus broke the remaining four commandments in reference to his relationship with God. So the Lord sent Nathan the prophet to reprove him (2 Samuel 12:1–13).

There is great significance in the order in which the reproof came. Nathan gave David (the shepherd of Israel) a parable about something that he could understand—sheep. He began with the natural realm, rather than immediately exposing the king's sin. He told a story about a rich man who, instead of taking a sheep from his own flock, killed a poor man's pet lamb to feed a stranger.

David was indignant, and sat up on his high throne of self-righteousness. He revealed his knowledge of the Law by saying that the guilty party would restore fourfold and would die for his crime. Nathan then exposed the king's sin of taking another man's "lamb," saying, "You are the man! ...Why have you despised the commandment of the Lord, to do evil in His sight?" When David cried, "I have sinned against the Lord!", the prophet *then* gave him grace and said, "The Lord also has put away your sin; you shall not die."

Imagine if Nathan, *fearful of rejection*, changed things around a little, and instead told David, "God loves you and has a wonderful plan for your life. However, there is something that is keeping you from enjoying this wonderful plan; it's called 'sin.'"

Imagine if he had glossed over the *personal nature* of David's sin, with a general reference to *all* men having sinned and fallen short of the glory of God. David's reaction may have been, "What *sin* are you talking about?" rather than to admit his terrible transgression. Think of it —why should he cry, *"I have sinned against the Lord!"* at the sound of *that* message? Instead, he may have, in a sincere desire to experience this "wonderful plan," admitted that he, like all men, had sinned and fallen short of the glory of God.

If David had not been made to *tremble* under the wrath of the Law, the prophet would have removed the very means of producing godly sorrow, which was so necessary for David's repentance. It is "godly sorrow" that produces repentance (2 Corinthians 7:10). It was the weight of his guilt that caused him to cry out, *"I have sinned against the Lord!"* The Law caused him to labor and become heavy laden; it made him hunger and thirst for righteousness. It enlightened him as to the *serious* nature of sin as far as God was concerned.

We received the following letter from someone who had listened to our teaching online and then tried using the Law in his preaching. He wrote: "I visited the Lebanon, Tennessee, prison system and witnessed to around thirty hardcore criminals in the maximum security area. I have never seen grown men cry like that!"

This letter came from Colorado: "God introduced me to your [teaching].[5] New power and anointing came my way and in preaching the Law over the last nine months or so, I have seen the fruit falling! Grown men crying, teens falling to their knees in front of their peers, and skeptics taking a new look."

Sin is like an onion. Its outer wrapper is a dry and crusty self-righteousness. It is only when its external casing is peeled away that it brings tears to the human eye. The Law peels the onion and allows contrition.

THE VASE

A child broke his father's antique vase. It was one that he was forbidden to touch, worth $25,000. However, the child thought the vase was merely worth $2, so he wasn't too concerned. He could easily replace it. It was only when he was later told of its true value that he saw the seriousness of his transgression and felt sorrow of heart. It was knowledge of the solemn nature of breaking an expensive antique, which he had been told not to touch, that enabled him to feel sorrow. If he had been left in ignorance of the value of the vase, he wouldn't have been truly sorry. Would you be upset if you had broken a vase you could easily replace?

The Law-less "God loves you and has a wonderful plan for your life" message doesn't cause the sinner to tremble. It doesn't show him the utterly serious nature of his transgression, so he doesn't find godly sorrow that produces repentance.

> *It was the weight of his guilt that caused David to cry out, "I have sinned against the Lord!"*

How true are these words spoken by Charles Spurgeon, the Prince of Preachers: "The Law serves a most necessary purpose." He said of sinners, "They will *never* accept grace until they tremble before a just and holy Law." Those who see the role of the Law will be Sons of Thunder *before* they are the Sons of Consolation. They know that the shoes of human pride must be removed before sinners can approach the burning bush of the gospel.

It is important to realize that we *can* evoke a tearful response from sinners by telling them that God loves them. The message is more appealing to both the Christian and the sinner. It is certainly easier to speak of love than to speak of sin. Many years ago, before I understood the function of God's Law, I told a prostitute of God's love and was delighted that she immediately began weeping. Unbeknown to me, her tears were not tears of godly sorrow for sin, but merely an emotional response to the need of a father's love.

In my ignorance, I joyfully led her in a sinner's prayer. However, I was disappointed some time later when she fell away, and her tender heart became *very* callous toward the things of God.

Paradoxical as it may seem, the Law makes grace abound, in the same way darkness makes light shine. It was John Newton, the writer of "Amazing Grace," who said that a wrong understanding of the harmony between Law and grace would produce "error on the left and the right hand." I don't know if any of us could claim to have a better understanding of grace than the one who penned such a hymn.

The question arises, Should a sinner be moved by Law or grace, by fear or love, when it comes to his salvation? We'll look at this in the next chapter.

FROM WHAT DID THEY FLEE?

9

I n 1993, the Washington, D.C. traffic authorities found themselves in a public dilemma. Members of a foreign embassy had been issued numerous parking tickets for breaking the law, but because their status made them immune to any form of prosecution, they therefore felt no obligation to pay for their violations. To that date, they owed the city six million dollars in unpaid fines.

What happened? They simply had no respect for the law, or for the agency of the law, *because there was no fear of future punishment.* They consequently became bold in their lawlessness.

However, in an effort to force them to pay their debts, authorities came up with a scheme where vehicles that were driven by traffic violators would not be able to be registered, so violators would therefore be unable to drive their cars.

The same thing has happened with the Church. It has failed to preach future punishment for violation of God's Law. Therefore sinners have become bold in their lawlessness. They have lost respect both for the Law and for its agency, the Church.

In San Diego, a strip club has a large sign that reads

"We didn't create sin, we just perfected it." One TV channel boasted of their adult programming: "Guaranteed to break more Commandments than any other lineup." A magazine cover in the Los Angeles Airport was headlined "Teenage Sex Romps. Stuff so bad, it's good. We're *so* ashamed." The secular world has become devoid of the fear of God; but how can they be expected to fear the Lord when much of the Church is offended by the concept? Unbeknown to them, they are daily clocking up debt to the Law, thinking that they will never have to pay the bill. They are storing up wrath that will be revealed in the Day of Wrath (Romans 2:5). If on that Day they are found in debt, they will pay for it with their souls. There will be hell to pay. Unless they are *convinced* that the Day of Reckoning is coming, that God will bring to judgment every secret thing, whether it is good or evil, they will continue to believe that God does not require an account.

Not Moved by Fear

L. E. Maxwell, Bible teacher and principal at the Prairie Bible Institute in Alberta, Canada, wrote of how students came to a knowledge of salvation. Some were "moved by fear"* and others were "moved by love." He noted that between 1931 and 1949, of the 2,507 students, nearly sixty-five percent were moved by fear, and only six percent were moved by love. The remaining twenty-nine percent came with another motive or couldn't remember why they came to the Savior.

> * This is an extremely important chapter. It deals with the wrath of God—an issue I seriously wrestled with when I first encountered this teaching. —KC

This side of Judgment Day, one can only surmise as to

how those not moved by fear ever found a place of repentance. This thought provokes the following inquiries:

- When they found a place of repentance, of what did they repent? It *must* have been "sin."

- When they understood that they had *sinned against God*, did they not fear at all? Didn't they have reverence enough for God to produce the fear of the Lord, which is the beginning of wisdom?

- When they turned from sin, how did they "flee from the wrath to come" without fear?

- If they were "moved by the love of God" seen in the cross, did they not fear at the extreme to which God went to redeem them because of their sin?

As Christians, have they yet come to a point of fearing God? What do they think when they read that God killed a husband and wife because they broke the Ninth Commandment (Acts 5:1–10)? Do they conclude that the psalmist was misguided when he wrote, "My flesh trembles for fear of You, and I am afraid of Your judgments" (Psalm 119:120)? Have they obeyed the command of Jesus: "I will show you whom you should fear: Fear Him who, after He has killed, has power to cast into hell; yes, I say to you, fear Him!" (Luke 12:5)? God provides a promise for those who do: "Blessed is every one who fears the LORD, who walks in His ways" (Psalm 128:1). Psalm 2:11 commands, "Serve the Lord with fear, and rejoice with trembling." The early Church did just that; they walked "in the fear of the Lord" (Acts 9:31).

How can the world be expected to fear the Lord when much of the Church is offended by the concept?

81

Scripture makes it very clear what it is that causes men to flee from sin. It's the "fear of the Lord" (Proverbs 16:6). Understandably, Maxwell's conclusion was not a concern that so many had fled to Christ in fear, *but that some hadn't*. When F. B. Meyer questioned four hundred Christian workers about why they came to Christ, "an overwhelming number testified that it was because of some message or influence of the terror of the Lord." The famous Bible teacher then said, "Oh, this is more than interesting and astonishing, especially in these days when we are rebuked often for not preaching more of the love of God!" R. C. Sproul said, "Jesus doesn't save us *to* God. He saves us *from* God." He also stated, "There's probably no concept in theology more repugnant to modern America than the idea of divine wrath."

If we minimize sin by downplaying it to sinners, we paint God as barbaric when we say that hell is the punishment for sin. This leads many believers to gloss over the mention of hell. Jesus on the other hand, did the opposite. He took the time to open up the Moral Law and show the sinner that the depth of his sin is "exceedingly sinful." By using the Moral Law to appeal to a man's conscience, Jesus made the sentence of eternal punishment reasonable and right in the eyes of the guilty party, thereby shining light upon his darkened mind. This gives the sinner a clear reason to repent and seek forgiveness through the mercy of the cross. —KC

Over the years that I have shared my concerns about contemporary evangelism, I have been careful never to name names. However, many have guessed that on occasion I have been referring to the incredibly popular tract *The Four Spiritual Laws*, penned by Dr. Bill Bright of Cam-

pus Crusade for Christ. More than a billion copies h
been distributed in all the major languages of the worl
and his approach has become the model for the modern
gospel presentation.

In July 2002, Kirk and I were invited to Orlando, Florida, to join Dr. Bright at his home for breakfast. After
breakfast, we sat down in his living room and heard this
warm, humble, sincere man of God confess (in his 81st
year) that he had been in error. Let me use his own words
from a book he wrote (published in July 2002) to tell you
what he said to us:

> In His approximately 42 months of public ministry,
> there are 33 recorded instances of Jesus speaking about
> hell. No doubt He warned of hell thousands of times.
> The Bible refers to hell a total of 167 times. I wonder
> with what frequency this eternal subject is found in today's pulpits. I confess I have failed in my ministry to
> declare the reality of hell as often as I have the love of
> God and the benefits of a personal relationship with
> Christ. But Jesus spent more of His time warning His
> listeners of the impending judgment of hell than speaking of the joys of heaven . . . I have never felt the need
> to focus on telling people about hell. However, as a
> result of a steady decline in morals and spiritual vitality
> in today's culture and a growing indifference to the afterlife, I have come to realize the need for greater discussion of hell . . . I have thus come to see that silence, or
> even benign neglect on these subjects, is disobedience
> on my part. To be silent on the eternal destinations of
> souls is to be like a sentry failing to warn his fellow soldiers of impending attack (*Heaven or Hell*, NewLife
> Publications, pp. 32, 48).

Dr. Bright even took the time to use the Law lawfully, by quoting every one of the Ten Commandments, then expounding the Law by saying, "Breaking these commandments will take us to hell without the intervening grace and mercy of Jesus Christ" (p. 37). In admitting "benign neglect on these subjects is disobedience on my part," such honesty reveals Dr. Bright's humility and his genuine love of the truth.

Please, follow his example and examine your evangelism in light of God's Word. At stake is the eternal salvation of millions of people. You don't need to throw away the *Four Spiritual Laws* method. Simply make four simple changes. First, don't tell the sinner that Jesus will improve his life. Second, don't make the unbiblical mistake of giving the cure before you convince of the disease. Third, take the time to follow in the footsteps of the Master by opening up the Commandments. And fourth, remember to faithfully include the terrible realities of Judgment Day and hell.

When I became a Christian, I was deeply touched by the love of God. Although I had sinned against God, He sent His Son to die for my sins and wanted a personal relationship with me! As I thought about these things, I came to the realization that if I had died that night I wouldn't have gone to heaven. I had ignored God my whole life. I not only didn't trust Him, I denied His very existence. There *was* an element of fear, but upon reflection, it was simply a fear that I wouldn't go to heaven.

The tragedy was that I had never shined the light of the Ten Commandments into the dark well of my heart and seen how deep the sinful waters were. I hadn't seen my own heart as "desperately wicked" and "deceitful above all things" (Jeremiah 17:9), so consequently it never dawned on me that God was angry with me—that I was actually an *enemy* of God because I had so greatly offended Him. The result of my shallow understanding of sin and hell paralyzed me from courageously reaching out to the lost—the very thing Jesus was most passionate about.

Those who come through the door of fear and trembling are made to perceive how ugly and offensive their sin really is to God. Therefore, they are now able to understand why God is angry with them and why hell is what they deserve. When people realize that God is offering salvation from His terrible wrath, gratitude for the Savior is infinitely deeper. The depth of their gratitude is in direct proportion to their perception of their sin. Shallow sorrow equals shallow gratitude.

Having a clear picture of hell has become a very effective motivator for me to run to the unsaved, to snatch them from the fire and bring them to the shelter of the cross.

Shortly after meeting Ray and understanding the reality of hell—and that no matter how good or kind a person perceives himself to be, he is headed for a place of eternal torment—I began to lose sleep. I had to do something. So I started talking about the things of God with more urgency and regularity. I'd think to myself, *What about the nice waitress in the restaurant? How can I in good conscience enjoy my meal, offer her a tip, and not even mention the dreadful fate she's heading toward unless she turns to Jesus?* I was sleepless over thoughts of people dying that very night, after I had told them to have a nice day but failed to give them the message that could have saved their eternal soul. I wanted to race back to the restaurant and write on a napkin the way of eternal life, and ask the waiters and waitresses to read it before they went home that night. I then realized that I would simply be writing my own gospel tract!

Maybe, like me, you have thought that passing out gospel tracts might do more harm than good. I used to see "freaks" out on street corners handing out "Jesus junk" to everyone who passed by, shoving their religious propaganda into people's faces. But now I recognize that there are also sane Christians who are passionate to reach the lost. I realized that tracts were a good thing. However, there are thoughtful, honest, effective tracts, and there are obnoxious, offensive, annoying tracts. I prefer those that reflect the heartfelt concern I have for people who don't know Jesus. Now I hand out tracts as often as I can and say, "This is for you. I'd really appreciate it if you'd take the time to read it. It has a gospel message inside." It may not be as good as a personal conversation, but at least it allows me to share the gospel with gentleness and respect.

I was recently enjoying a day at the beach in Southern California. I noticed a lifeguard in his wooden hut talking on the phone. After he finished, I went over and introduced myself, and thanked him for watching out for our safety. I then asked him, "If you were talking on the phone and you noticed someone drowning, could you in good conscience turn away and let him sink to his death so that you could continue your phone conversation?" He said, "Of course not!" Then I explained that, just as he would do anything in his power to save the life of a drowning victim, I too needed to give him something to think about. I asked him to please read the tract. With a puzzled look, he told me he would and said, "Thanks."

Since I've become passionate about reaching the lost, I realized that the gospel on paper is infinitely better than no gospel at all. Also, I've had many people come back after receiving a tract and tell me that they really appreciated it because it made them reconsider their spiritual beliefs. If you don't like any of the tracts you've seen in the past, try our unique tracts (view them at www.livingwaters.com)—or grab a napkin and write your own! What's important is that you do something to reach out to the lost. —*KC*

WELL-VERSED

As I was waiting to witness to a couple, I couldn't help but hear some of the filthy language a young lady was using to describe a situation that displeased her. When I found a gap in the conversation, I gave them a couple of our tracts, along with two pennies with the Ten Commandments pressed into them, and swung the conversation to the Law. The young lady with the dirty mouth claimed she was a Christian, but when I said that I had heard her language and that something wasn't right, she admitted she was a "backslider." She was very well-versed in the knowledge of the way of salvation, but she was adamant that one should not come to Christ because of the fear of "Judgment Day, hell, or the wrath of God." She said that we should come to Christ because of God's love, expressed in the cross.

It was obvious by her sinful lifestyle that she had mere head knowledge of God's love. She didn't consider it a love worthy of her attention. When I told her, "Jesus said, 'Don't fear him who has power to kill your body, and afterward can do no more. But fear Him who has power to kill the body and cast your soul into hell; fear Him,'" then she said, "I think that you were sent to me today."

A. W. Tozer wrote in *The Knowledge of the Holy*:

> God's justice stands forever against the sinner in utter severity. The vague and tenuous hope that God is

too kind to punish the ungodly has become a deadly opiate for the consciences of millions. It hushes their fears and allows them to practice all pleasant forms of iniquity while death draws every day nearer and the command to repent goes unregarded. As responsible moral beings, we dare not so trifle with our eternal future.

A close friend of mine told me that as a professing Christian he lacked the fear of God. To him, God was just a good friend. One day he found out that his girlfriend's parents were out of town. He immediately dropped to his knees and earnestly prayed, "Lord, this could be of You. I want to lose my virginity today. I will know it's of You if she says to come on over." She invited him over and he became a fornicator that day. Then he earnestly thanked God for what he saw as the Lord giving him his heart's desire.

He found a place of genuine repentance some time later, and is now soundly saved and fervently serving God.

A lack of the fear of God isn't confined to the pews. Almost 40 percent of *pastors* who were polled admitted that they'd had an extramarital affair since beginning their ministry.

Those who lack the fear of God will not stop at fornication. A wise man once said, "Most I fear God. Next to Him, I fear him that fears Him not." If someone has no fear of God, he will lie to you, steal from you, and even kill you . . . if he thinks he can get away with it.

How Many Lies?

A six-year-old boy once approached his father, who, as a pastor, understood the importance of a sinner having knowledge of sin. The child said that he wanted to "ask Jesus into his heart." The father, suspecting that the child lacked the knowledge of sin, told him that he could do so when he was older, then sent him off to bed.

A short time later, the boy got out of bed and asked his father if he could give his life to the Savior. The father still wasn't persuaded of the son's understanding, and not wanting the child's salvation to be spurious, he sent him back to his room. A third time the son returned. This time the father questioned him about whether he had broken any of the Ten Commandments. The young boy didn't think he had. When he was asked if he had lied, the child said that he hadn't. The father thought for a moment, then asked him how many lies he had to tell to be a liar. When it was established that one lie made a person a liar, the child realized he had lied, and broke down in uncontrollable tears. When the father then asked him if he wanted to ask Jesus into his heart, the child *cringed* and nodded his head. He was cringing because he now had a knowledge that he had sinned against God. That produced fear. At this point, he could do more than experimentally "ask Jesus into his heart." He could find a place of godly sorrow. Even at his young age, he could exercise repentance toward the God he now understood that he had offended.

> *"The vague and tenuous hope that God is too kind to punish the ungodly has become a deadly opiate for millions."*

After speaking of the importance of the place of fear, L. E. Maxwell said:

> Is the majesty of the Moral Ruler to meet with no respect? Is the authority of His Law of no consequence? Is there nothing in God to fear? An effete dilettantism would feign tell us so. Nevertheless all history and Scrip-

ture and experience cry out against such an emasculated and effeminate theology.

It is the fear of God that should stop the Christian from flirting with the eternal well-being of sinners by diluting the message with which he has been entrusted. His devotion to the truth will be rewarded: "Those who rebuke the wicked will have delight, and a good blessing will come upon them" (Proverbs 24:25).

It seems that John Wesley had those in his day who refused to preach the Law to bring the knowledge of sin. They justified their method by saying that they preached "Christ and Him crucified." So Wesley pointed to Paul's method of preaching Christ crucified:

> *To persuade sinners "concerning Jesus," Paul used both prophecy and the Law of Moses.*

When Felix sent for Paul, on purpose that he might "hear him concerning the faith in Christ;" instead of preaching Christ in *your* sense (which would probably have caused the Governor either to mock or to contradict and blaspheme,) "he reasoned of righteousness, temperance, and judgment to come," till Felix (hardened as he was) "trembled" (Acts 24:24,25). Go thou and tread in his steps. Preach Christ to the careless sinner, by reasoning "of righteousness, temperance, and judgment to come!"

The Bible gives us further insight into Paul's reasoning. In Acts 28:23 we read, "When they had appointed him a day, many came to him at his lodging, to whom he explained and solemnly testified of the kingdom of God, persuading them concerning Jesus from both the Law of Moses and the Prophets, from morning till evening."

Our aim in preaching is to persuade sinners "concerning Jesus." *He* is the way, the truth, and the life. Without Him they will perish. How does Paul do that? He used *both* prophecy and the Law of Moses. Prophecy appeals to a man's intellect and creates faith in the Word of God. As he realizes that the Bible is no ordinary book—that it contains hundreds of indisputable prophecies that substantiate its supernatural origin—he begins to give Scripture credibility. However, the Law of Moses appeals to a man's *conscience* and brings the knowledge of sin. Paul used both because prophecy doesn't bring an awareness of sin.

A NEW GOSPEL PRESENTATION

A well-known charismatic couple, whose aim is to reach millions with the gospel, say that they have discovered a new method to get people saved. They maintain that an angel told the woman how to get instant decisions. Let's assume that you are in a restaurant and you want a waitress to make a decision for Christ. This is what you would say:

"Do you know there are two kinds of beautiful waitresses?" Her answer: "Really?" Then you say, "Yes! Those who are saved and those who are about to be. Which one are you?" If her answer is anything other than, "I am saved," say, "Repeat this after me: 'Father, forgive my sins. Jesus, come into my heart. Make me the kind of person You want me to be. Thank You for saving me.'" Now, ask the person: "Where is Jesus right now?" If she answers, "In my heart," say, "Congratulations on being a child of God!" If her answer is anything else, have her repeat the prayer after you again.

The couple also insist, "When you talk to someone, use the same words the angel said. It works! If you change the words, it does not work!"

This technique that the "angel" gave the woman isn't new. It is the age-old selling approach of manipulating a customer so he will answer in the way you want him to. However, there is one important difference. Waitresses are trained to be congenial to customers—not only for the sake of their job, but because the size of their tip depends on it.

Why would an angel of God, after 2,000 years of evangelism, suddenly announce a method that isn't in line with God's revealed Word? Did God suddenly figure out a new way to reach the lost, and then send His angel to tell us? Did He change His mind about how to reach the world?

If an angel tells us of a gospel (or a method of gospel promotion) that isn't in line with Holy Scripture, we should reject it without a second thought. Why would we do such a thing, even if it *seemed* to work? Simply because we fear God in light of the apostle Paul's sober warning in Galatians 1:8: "But even if we, *or an angel from heaven*, preach any other gospel to you than what we have preached to you, let him be accursed" (emphasis added).

Again, I cannot express my anguish over this type of "evangelism." My heart's cry is for people to be saved from hell, and yet modern methods work *against*, not *for* that end. Dare I say it, but they are doing the *devil's* work rather than the Lord's. In Matthew 13:25 we are told, "While men slept, his enemy came and sowed tares among the wheat and went his way." As Christians we must be alert to the workings of the enemy, understand about true and false conversions, and fear God enough to follow in the steps of *biblical* evangelism.* We should heed Paul's warning against "peddling God's Word [shortchanging and adulterating the divine message]" (2 Corinthians 2:17, Amplified). John Wesley said that those who didn't bother to use the Law were either "babes in Christ, or strangers to regeneration."

* Feel free to check out "The Way of the Master Academy," our comprehensive school of biblical evangelism. Go to www.livingwaters.com and click on "Academy." —KC

A pastor of a large church in the South told me that almost everyone in the "Bible Belt" parrots the same phrase. As soon as individuals are personally challenged about their salvation they say, "I have received Jesus Christ as Lord and Savior. I've dealt with that," and yet he knows in his heart of hearts that there are no signs of regeneration. He said that it's as though they have been inoculated against the truth. *They have.*

I received the following letter from a very concerned mother:

> It was at a youth camp that my oldest son "gave his heart to Jesus" and was baptized, but since then has shown no real desire that I can see to live for the Lord. I don't want to seem critical, but I just don't see the desire in any way, shape, or form. I don't want to see the same thing happen with my other two kids.

God only knows how many others have had the experience of seeing false professions of loved ones. When these false converts fall away, they become bitter, and their latter end becomes *worse* than the first. They are *inoculated* against the truth. What can this mother now say to her son?

I deal with so many who are more than fruitless converts, they are venomous "backsliders." They have enough ammunition to do great damage to the cause of the gospel. Yet, as they pour out their hatred and filthy blasphemy, my heart goes out to them because they are the sad product of manipulative modern methods.

The next time you find someone who is into the occult or some weird cult, dig a little, and then don't be surprised when you find that they once "gave their heart to Jesus." Scripture warns that many false converts will leave the church: "Now the Spirit expressly says that in latter times *some will depart from the faith*, giving heed to deceiving spirits and doctrines of demons" (1 Timothy 4:1, emphasis added).

THE DRIVING POWER

Charles Spurgeon reiterates the importance of stressing the coming Day of Judgment:

> God [has] appointed a Day in which He will judge the world, and we sigh and cry until it shall end the reign of wickedness, and give rest to the oppressed. Brethren, we must preach the coming of the Lord, and preach it somewhat more than we have done; *because it is the driving power of the gospel.* Too many have kept back these truths, and thus the bone has been taken out of the arm of the gospel. Its point has been broken; its edge has been blunted. The doctrine of judgment to come is the power by which men are to be aroused. There is another life; the Lord will come a second time; judgment will arrive; the wrath of God will be revealed. *Where this is not preached, I am bold to say the gospel is not preached.* It is absolutely necessary to the preaching of the gospel of Christ that men be warned as to what will happen if they continue in their sins.
>
> Ho, ho sir surgeon, you are too delicate to tell the man that he is ill! You hope to heal the sick without their knowing it. You therefore flatter them; and what happens? They laugh at you; they dance upon their own graves. At last they die! Your delicacy is cruelty; your flatteries are poisons; *you are a murderer.* Shall we keep men in a fool's paradise? Shall we lull them into

soft slumbers from which they will awake in hell? Are we to become helpers of their damnation by our smooth speeches? In the name of God we will not.

In *Striking Incidents of Saving Grace*, Henry Breeden tells of a preacher in Colliery, England, who saw a number of conversions take place under his ministry. Then in 1861 a "stranger" passed through and conducted meetings in which "there were great numbers of persons" who professed faith in Jesus. The preacher then recounts the sad effects:

> But many of them were, in a short time, gone back again into the world. Indeed, so complete was the failure that the Minister who succeeded me in that Circuit said, "There was not one single person, out of about ninety who professed to obtain Religion through that man's services, that continued to be a member of the Colliery Church."
>
> I had observed the same sort of thing before in regard to the efforts of suchlike persons in other places. And, therefore, I was very desirous to find out what was the cause of such failures. I was sure that the persons, said to be brought in under my own ministry, had nearly all of them held on their way, and were then members—either in the Church above, or in the Church below. So I set myself calmly to consider the whole affair. In doing this, I soon found that the preaching that does not address the sinner's conscience, and strive to break the unconverted spirit down by enforcing the Law of God, scarcely ever leads to the salvation of the soul. And these men scarcely ever preach the Law.
>
> Yes, that is it, and nothing else—"By the Law is the knowledge of sin." Let a minister get that important sentiment burnt into his very soul by the Light and flaming Love of God. And then let him go forth and preach

the truth as it is in Jesus, and many, many precious souls will soon be saved. But let him omit preaching the Law, and whatever else he may do—for he can accomplish many great things—yet, under that man's ministry, conversions will be scarce (Harvey Christian Publishers, pp. 188,189).

I couldn't give a more hearty "Amen!" to his conclusion: "Yes, that is it, and nothing else—'By the Law is the knowledge of sin.'" This teaching is so foundational, and yet we have failed to see its simple truth.

When I first grasped the concept of using the Law in witnessing, I was thrilled to have the feather duster of modern evangelism replaced with the Ten Great Cannons. As I understood the function of the Law to bring a person to the cross in humility and brokenness, I wondered if the message of grace had somehow been lost in the process. Other Christian friends often reminded me of the truth that we are "saved by grace, not by the Law." Where was the love in telling people that they have violated God's Laws and would therefore go to hell? Does the Law save them? No! Will the fear of God's wrath save them? Never!

The beauty of the Law is that it breaks the proud heart and shows the man his guilt before God. Once a man has been broken and his sin exposed before God, he can see his need for mercy and forgiveness. He is no longer proud and arrogant, but rather humbled and thirsty for the kindness and mercy God offers in the cross. With an understanding that *death* is what he deserves, he can now appreciate that "God demonstrates His own love toward us, in that while we were still sinners, Christ died for us" (Romans 5:8). Now the man can truly appreciate the precious blood of Christ that saves him.

The harsh demands of God's Law *magnify* His free gift of grace. Once the light of the Law shone on my heart, I was horrified, embarrassed, and ashamed—I had violated it terribly. But then, as clear as day, I could see the beauty of the cross! The Law *magnified* my thirst for Jesus. I finally understood why Jesus is the only way to the Father (John 14:6). I am deeply grateful for what the Law did to drive me and glue me to the Savior.

Without the Law, the message of Jesus on the cross will not make sense. Taking chemotherapy if you don't think you have cancer would be foolish. Surrendering your life to Jesus when you don't think it's necessary is like selling your house to pay for a crime you don't think you've committed. Without knowledge of the Law, the masses will perceive Jesus' death as the unfortunate fate of a good man, the just punishment of a religious lunatic, or simply an ancient legend. But with an understanding of God's Law, they can *clearly see* and *fully understand* that He is their only hope of ever going to heaven.

The Law enables grace to make sense. If I don't understand that I've broken the law, then someone telling me I'm going to jail seems unreasonable. If I don't think I deserve to go to jail, I won't appreciate the judge offering to post my bail. I may think it's a kind gesture, but completely out of line, because I don't think I should have been arrested in the first place. I'd appeal the case, defend myself, and accuse the prosecution of harassment. In the same way, if a person doesn't think he's guilty and deserves hell, he won't fall on his face and beg God for mercy and forgiveness. He won't appreciate Jesus' blood being shed for him, because he doesn't think he needs it.

If there is no conviction of guilt, there's no confession and no repentance. But if the criminal clearly understands that he is guilty of breaking the law and knows he is deeply indebted to it, then he might humbly admit his guilt, confess his crimes, and ask the judge for mercy.

God gave us the Ten Commandments to show us that we have violated an Eternal Law, offended the Judge of the Universe, and will be guilty when tried in the Court of No Compromise. Only when a sinner *actually perceives* that he deserves punishment in hell will he fall on his knees like the man in the temple, and say, "God, be merciful to me a sinner!" Only when a man understands the filth of his own heart will he cling with all his might to the cleansing power of the cross and never let go. Only when he sees himself naked before the eyes of an all-seeing God will he treasure the pure white robe of the righteousness of Christ.

The problem with omitting the Law when witnessing is that most men and women think that they're good people, believing that their own good deeds will be enough to earn them a place in heaven. But the Bible says that, even though "there is none who does good, no, not one," still, each man will proclaim his own goodness. It's true! The majority of people (including most professing Christians) consider themselves to be "good."

Look at Luke 18:18 to see what Jesus said to a man who inquired about eternal life. Jesus used the Law to expose this man's sin of idolatry (his god was his money) and to bring an awareness of his need for forgiveness. Shouldn't we follow in the Master's footsteps? Jesus used the Law when He witnessed to a proud, self-righteous sinner. Only when He was talking with an already humbled, repentant person (like the thief on the cross and

Nicodemus) did He simply share the good news of God's grace. Jesus wasn't eliminating grace from the way of salvation; He simply knew that the Law was designed for hardhearted sinners—to *prepare the way* for the gospel of grace. —KC

In the next chapter we are going to look at the importance of a sinner's motive in his response to the gospel.

THE MOTIVE
AND THE RESULT

L et me now share with you a portion of a teaching I often give which tends to clarify the motive sinners should have when they come to the Savior.

Two men are seated in a plane. The first is given a parachute and told to put it on, as it would improve his flight. He's a little skeptical at first, since he can't see how wearing a parachute in a plane could possibly improve his flight.

After some time, he decides to experiment and see if the claims are true. As he puts it on, he notices the weight of it upon his shoulders and he finds he has difficulty in sitting upright. However, he consoles himself with the fact that he was told the parachute would improve his flight. So he decides to give it a little time.

As he waits, he notices that some of the other passengers are laughing at him because he's wearing a parachute in a plane. He begins to feel somewhat humiliated. As they continue to laugh and point at him, he can stand it no longer. He sinks in his seat, unstraps the parachute, and throws it to the floor. Disillusionment and bitterness fill his heart, because as far as he was concerned he was told an outright lie.

The second man is given a parachute, *but listen to what*

he is told. He's told to put it on because at any moment he'll be jumping 25,000 feet out of the plane. He gratefully puts the parachute on. He doesn't notice the weight of it upon his shoulders, nor that he can't sit upright. His mind is consumed with the thought of what would happen to him if he jumped without the parachute.

Let's now analyze the *motive* and the *result* of each passenger's experience. The first man's motive for putting on the parachute was solely to improve his flight. The result of his experience was that he was humiliated by the passengers, disillusioned, and somewhat embittered against those who gave him the parachute. As far as he's concerned, it will be a long time before anyone gets one of those things on his back again.

> If we are true and faithful witnesses, that's what we'll be preaching—that there is wrath to come.

The second man put on the parachute solely to escape the jump to come. And because of his knowledge of what would happen to him if he jumped without it, he has a deep-rooted joy and peace in his heart knowing that he's saved from sure death. This knowledge gives him the ability to withstand the mockery of the other passengers. His attitude toward those who gave him the parachute is one of heartfelt gratitude.

Listen to what the modern gospel says: "Put on the Lord Jesus Christ. He'll give you love, joy, peace, fulfillment, and lasting happiness." In other words, Jesus will improve your flight. The sinner responds, and in an experimental fashion puts on the Savior to see if the claims are true. And what does he get? The promised temptation, tribulation, and persecution—the other passengers mock him. So what does he do? He takes off the Lord Jesus Christ; he's offended for the

Word's sake; he's disillusioned and somewhat embittered; and quite rightly so. He was promised peace, joy, love, and fulfillment, and all he got were trials and humiliation. His bitterness is directed toward those who gave him the so-called "good news." His latter end becomes worse than the first—he's another inoculated and bitter "backslider."

Instead of preaching that Jesus improves the flight, we should be warning the passengers that they have to jump out of a plane. That it's appointed for man to die once, and after this the judgment. When a sinner understands the horrific consequences of breaking the Law of God, he will flee to the Savior solely to escape the wrath that's to come. If we are true and faithful witnesses, that's what we'll be preaching—that there is wrath to come—that "God commands all men everywhere to repent, *because* He has appointed a day on which He will judge the world in righteousness" (Acts 17:30,31, emphasis added). The issue isn't one of happiness, but one of righteousness.

It doesn't matter how happy a sinner is, or how much he is enjoying the pleasures of sin for a season; without the righteousness of Christ, he will perish on the day of wrath. The Bible says, "Riches do not profit in the day of wrath, but righteousness delivers from death" (Proverbs 11:4). Peace and joy are legitimate *fruits* of salvation, but it's not legitimate to use these fruits as a drawing card *for* salvation. If we do so, the sinner will respond with an impure motive, lacking repentance.

Can you remember why the *second* passenger had joy and peace in his heart? It was because he knew that the parachute was going to save him from sure death. In the same way, as believers, we have joy and peace in believing because we know that the righteousness of Christ is going to deliver us from the wrath that is to come.

With that thought in mind, let's take a close look at an incident aboard the plane. We have a brand new flight attendant. It's her first day, and she's carrying a tray of boiling hot coffee. She wants to leave an impression on the passengers and she certainly does! As she's walking down the aisle, she trips over someone's foot and slops the hot coffee all over the lap of our second passenger. What's his reaction as that boiling liquid hits his tender flesh? Does he say, "Man, that hurt!"? Yes, he does. But then does he rip the parachute from his shoulders, throw it to the floor, and say, "That stupid parachute!"? No; why should he? He didn't put the parachute on for a better flight. He put it on to save him from the jump to come. If anything, the hot coffee incident causes him to cling tighter to the parachute and even look forward to the jump.

If we have put on the Lord Jesus Christ for the right motive—to flee from the wrath to come—then when tribulation strikes, when the flight gets bumpy, we won't get angry at God, and we won't lose our joy and peace. Why should we? We didn't come to Christ for a better lifestyle, but to flee from the wrath to come.

If anything, tribulation drives the true believer *closer* to the Savior. Sadly, multitudes of professing Christians lose their joy and peace when the flight gets bumpy. Why? Because they are the product of a man-centered gospel. They came lacking repentance, without which we cannot be saved.

WHAT WAS PHARAOH'S PROBLEM?

Why did it take so long for Pharaoh to bow to the will of the God of Israel? One would think that one plague would have caused him to immediately let God's people go. The answer is given to us in Exodus 9:27,28. After a number of terrible plagues, Pharaoh called for Moses and Aaron and said, "I have sinned this time. The Lord is righteous, and my people and I are wicked. Entreat the Lord, that there may be no more mighty thundering and hail, for it is enough. I will let you go, and you shall stay no longer." Such talk would seem to show that finally he was repentant. However, Exodus 9:30 gives insight as to what was still lacking. Moses said, "But as for you and your servants, I know that you will not yet fear the Lord God." Pharaoh saw his sin as something he had done "this time," and in his heart he didn't yet fear God enough to obey Him.

There are many who profess faith in the Savior who are like Pharaoh. A lack of knowledge of the Law has left them with a shallow understanding as to the exceedingly sinful nature of sin. They admit that they

We didn't come to Christ for a better lifestyle, but to flee from the wrath to come.

sinned "this time." They think sin is something they have done, rather than something that saturates their very nature. They lack the fear of God, and, like Pharaoh, these "believers" entreat the Lord simply because they find themselves in the midst of thunderous trials. Then, like the king of Egypt, when the plagues of life stop, they sin once again and harden their hearts to the will of God (Exodus 9:34).

What is it, then, that will break the will of a stubborn, rebellious sinner who gives mere lip service to God, but doesn't fear Him? The answer is, not only does he need to be terrified by the plagues of God's Law, but he also must see the death of the Firstborn. After the Law has done its terrifying work, the gospel will then give him light regarding the cost of his redemption. His heart will fear when he realizes that his liberty from wrath came through the death of the firstborn Son of God.

However, the death of Jesus of Nazareth, which purchased our salvation, didn't come swiftly. Jesus Himself told us that "Christ must suffer." When commenting on Psalm 22:14, Charles Spurgeon said:

> The placing of the cross in its socket had shaken Him with great violence, had strained all the ligaments, pained every nerve, and more or less dislocated all His bones. Burdened with His own weight, the august sufferer felt the strain increasing every moment of those six long hours. His sense of faintness and general weakness were overpowering; while to His own consciousness He became nothing but a mass of misery and swooning sickness... To us, sensations such as our Lord endured would have been insupportable, and kind unconsciousness would have come to our rescue; but in His case, He was wounded, and felt the sword; He drained the cup and tasted every drop.

The risen Savior retained the scars of the cross for a reason. Calvary's grisly wounds must remain before the eyes of the Christian. They stand as a fearful testimony, not only of God's unfathomable love for sinners, but of His incredible love for justice.

As I began to understand the use of the Law to bring repentance, the question arose in my mind, "But if we tell unbelievers about the Law, sin, righteousness, judgment, hell, and *then* the cross, are we under-emphasizing God's love and grace? After all, isn't love what the gospel is all about?" A few good friends have also asked me this question, and I am grateful for their bluntness because it cuts to the chase.

The Bible consistently defines the love of God toward

sinners in two words: *the cross.*

- "For God so loved the world that *He gave His only begotten Son*" (John 3:16).

- "But God demonstrates His own love toward us, in that while we were still sinners, *Christ died for us*" (Romans 5:8).

- "Live a life of love, just as *Christ loved us and gave himself up for us* as a fragrant offering and sacrifice to God" (Ephesians 5:2, NIV).

- "By this we know love, because *He laid down His life for us*" (1 John 3:16).

- "This is love: not that we loved God, but that He loved us and *sent His Son as an atoning sacrifice for our sins*" (1 John 4:10, NIV).

Always and without fail, God uses the cross as the supreme example of His love toward sinners. Sure, God expresses His love toward *the saved believer* by offering daily comfort, joy, inner peace, patience, self-control, and a safe harbor in times of trouble, but never does He offer these to the unbeliever. Check it out yourself. Look in your Bible to find any instance of Jesus, an apostle, or a prophet offering an unrepentant sinner any form of God's love other than Jesus' blood on the cross. Rather, God's wrath is on them! The cross is love's masterpiece. The cross is God motivated by love, running toward the sinner to rescue him from the flames of eternal punishment.

If I were to pinpoint a time in my life when my earthly father clearly demonstrated his love for me, it would be the time he saved my life. I was four years old, playing on a boat dock, when I fell into the water and was drowning. I likely would have died if my father had not been there to save me. He dived into the water and rescued me. I know that my father loves me *because he saved my life*. I couldn't want better proof that my father loves me than the fact that he risked his own life to save mine, and every other demonstration of love pales in comparison to that supreme moment of mercy.

So when it comes to telling sinners about the heavenly Father's love, if we have to point beyond the cross where Jesus rescued them from the waters of eternal death, we are missing the focal point of God's love. If you feel the simple message of the cross is not enough to describe the love of God, will you say that to the Father who sacrificed His one and only Son, or to Jesus who loved you and gave His own life for you, or to the countless martyrs who died simply because Jesus loved them and died for them? To promise an unsaved sinner anything more than the full mercy and compassion of the cross is to go beyond Scripture. As Paul said to the sinful Corinthians, "I determined not to know anything among you *except Jesus Christ and Him crucified*" (1 Corinthians 2:2, emphasis added).

Perhaps the problem isn't that sinners need more than "Christ crucified," but that they need to hear a better explanation of the One who loved us and gave Himself up for us. As messengers of life to a dying world, we must point people to Jesus and magnify the love of God in Him. We must expound the love that held Jesus to the cross, and fill the mind of the unsaved with the knowledge of God's solemn promise, written with His own blood, to forgive those who believe in Jesus. God help us to faithfully proclaim the full love of God in the cross.

Believer, do you understand that love yourself? Do

you understand what you were saved from? Have you ever looked for yourself into the mirror of God's Law and seen your own heart's exceedingly sinful reflection? Do you know how hot the flames burn in God's eternal prison? Have you ever wept tears of gratitude for the precious blood of Jesus spilled to save you? If not, you will no doubt find it difficult to explain the cross to others.

These are sobering thoughts for me as well as for anyone who has not yet fled to the Savior to escape the wrath to come. A fool will dismiss them as judgmental, but a wise person will examine himself to see if he is in the faith (2 Corinthians 13:5). —KC

In the next chapter, we are going to draw from the wisdom of men whose results the Church admires, but of whose methods many are sadly ignorant.

EXPERIENCE, THE TRUE TEST

L et's now draw on the experiential wisdom of eminent men of God of the past. Martin Luther, in his commentary on Galatians, wrote: "Satan, the god of all dissension, stirreth up daily new sects, and last of all, which of all other I should never have foreseen or once suspected, he hath raised up a sect as such as teach...that men should not be terrified by the Law, but gently exhorted by the preaching of the grace of Christ." He was speaking of what he perceived as a satanic doctrine that was invading the Church of his day—a "sect" had risen which teaches that men should not be terrified by the Law, but gently exhorted by the preaching of the grace of Christ. His words perfectly describe the methods of most of contemporary evangelism. Modern evangelists would never think of using the Law to terrify, but instead, they prefer to gently exhort by preaching the grace of Christ. Luther further stated, "The true function of the Law is to accuse and to kill; but the function of the gospel is to make alive."

While the Law serves as a moral guide to genuine believers, its primary function is to kill and destroy self-righteousness. All hope in our own good works must be put to death if we are ever to depend upon Jesus, who alone can bring life. The Law brings that necessary death. —KC

In his book *Holiness*, J. C. Ryle wrote of the sinner's motivation in coming to Christ:

People will never set their faces decidedly towards heaven, and live like pilgrims, until they really feel that they are in danger of hell...Let us expound and beat out the Ten Commandments, and show the length, and breadth, and depth, and height of their requirements.[6] This is the way of our Lord in the Sermon on the Mount. We cannot do better than follow His plan. We may depend on it, men will never come to Jesus, and stay with Jesus, and live for Jesus, unless they really know why they are to come, and what is their need. Those whom the Spirit draws to Jesus are those whom the Spirit has convinced of sin. Without thorough conviction of sin, men may seem to come to Jesus and follow Him for a season, but they will soon fall away and return to the world.

Dr. Martyn Lloyd-Jones spoke of the function of God's Law in gospel proclamation:

The trouble with people who are not seeking for a Savior, and for salvation, is that they do not understand the nature of sin. It is the peculiar function of the Law to bring such an understanding to a man's mind and conscience. That is why great evangelical preachers 300 years ago in the time of the Puritans, and 200 years ago in the time of Whitefield and others, always engaged in what they called a preliminary "Law work."

John R. W. Stott, commenting on Galatians 3:23–29,

said, "We cannot come to Christ to be justified until we have first been to Moses, to be condemned. But once we have gone to Moses, and acknowledged our sin, guilt and condemnation, we must not stay there. We must let Moses send us to Christ."

SOME CONCERNS

Let me take a moment to address some questions that may have arisen in your mind.

Romans 2:4 tells us that it is "the goodness of God leads [us] to repentance." Some try to use this verse to justify a message devoid of sin, righteousness, and judgment, saying that we need merely speak of God's goodness to see sinners saved. However, it should be pointed out that this verse is sandwiched between some of the harshest statements of God's judgment and wrath. If Paul was saying that we should speak only of God's goodness to sinners, he wasn't practicing what he preached. The great hymnwriter Isaac Watts said, "I never knew but one person in the whole course of my ministry who acknowledged that the first motions of religion in his own heart arose from a sense of the goodness of God, 'What shall I render to the Lord, who has dealt so bountifully with me?' But I think all besides who have come within my notice have rather been first awakened to fly from the wrath to come by the passion of fear."

I hope that you don't get the impression that I'm suggesting that we preach only God's judgment, and never give sinners the message of grace. The truth is that we must continually preach God's love shown in the cross. That is the focus. We are *determined* to preach Christ, and Him crucified. When we are witnessing and preaching, John 3:16 is where we should be heading, but we must make sure that we get to it down Biblical Avenue.

I also hope you don't think that my asking someone if they are good or have lied or stolen, etc., is my method. As much as I would like to take the credit for such a wonderfully effective way of awakening sinners, I can't. I learned it from the greatest Evangelist. It is the way of the Master to correct sinners regarding their understanding of the word "good," and to ask if they have kept the Commandments (see Jesus use it in Luke 18:20).

To see real-life witnessing, see "The Way of the Master" video series at www.livingwaters.com. —KC

Those modern evangelists who may be tempted to discard this teaching because they think it is simply a "method" should also then consider their ways. Can the rehearsed catch phrases used while preaching, having counselors come forward first to draw out decisions—heads bowed, eyes closed, music playing, etc.—be shown to be biblical, or are they manmade methods used to get decisions? We should determine our evangelistic traditions solely in light of holy Scripture.

THE CONSCIENCE BEARS WITNESS

A Nazi soldier was once questioned about why he mercilessly shot Jewish women and children during World War II. He told the interviewer that one of the motivations was "curiosity." He calmly said, "I just fired and they fell." When the interviewer asked if he felt bad about doing such things, he said, "I was given 20 years, and I served 20 years." In other words, he had paid his debt to society for his misdeeds. The scales were now balanced. Justice had been served.

However, when the interviewer asked him about his conscience, he refused to speak any further, and immediately terminated the interview. Conscience speaks of more than guilt for transgressions of *civil* law. The conscience bears witness to the Moral Law. It reminds men that there is a God whose Law we have transgressed.

Paris Reidhead said these wonderfully wise words:

> If I had my way, I would declare a moratorium on public preaching of "the plan of salvation" in America for one to two years. Then I would call on everyone who has use of the airwaves and the pulpits to preach the holiness of God, the righteousness of God and the Law of God, until sinners would cry out, "What must we do to be saved?" Then I would take them off in a corner and whisper the gospel to them. Such drastic action is needed because we have gospel-hardened a generation of sinners by telling them how to be saved before they have any understanding why they need to be saved.
>
> Don't use John 3:16. Why? Because you tell a sinner how to be saved before he has realized that he needs to be saved. What you have done is gospel-hardened him.

What did he say? *"Don't use John 3:16."* That sounds like heresy! Of course, we should use John 3:16; it should be the focal point of the gospel. He is simply saying that we should not prescribe the cure before we have convinced of the disease. D. L. Moody said:

> It is a great mistake to give a man who has not been convicted of sin certain passages that were never meant for him. The Law is what he needs...Do not offer the consolation of the gospel until he sees and knows he is guilty before God. We must give enough of the Law to take away all self-righteousness. I pity the man who preaches only one side of the truth—always the gospel,

and never the Law (*Pleasures and Profit of Bible Study*, Morgan and Scott Ltd., p. 111).

THE LIGHT DIDN'T WAKEN HIM

Peter lay soundly asleep in Herod's prison (Acts 12:6). This is faith in action. Faith snoozes, even in a storm. Stephen had been stoned, James had just been killed with a sword—and Peter sleeps like a parishioner in the back row of a dead church. He was bound with chains between two soldiers. More guards stood before the door of the prison. Suddenly an angel of the Lord appeared and stood by him, "and a light shone in the cell." There is a strong inference that the light didn't awaken Peter from his sleep, because the Scriptures then tell us that the angel struck him on the side. As he arose, his chains fell off, he girded himself, tied on his shoes, put on his garment, and followed the angel. After that, the iron gate leading to the city opened of its own accord, and Peter was free.

The sinner is in the prison of his sins. He is taken captive by the devil. He is bound by the chains of sin, under the sentence of death. He is asleep in his sins. He lives in a dream world. But it isn't the gospel light that will awaken him. How can "Good News" alarm a sinner? No, the Law must strike him. He needs to be struck with the lightning of Sinai and awakened by its thunderings. That will rouse him to his plight of being on the threshold of death. Then he will arise and the gospel will remove the chains of sin and death. It will be "the power of God to salvation." Then he will gird himself with truth, tie on his gospel shoes, put on his garment of righteousness, follow the Lord, and the iron gate of the Celestial City will open of its own accord.

Our nation is full of people—both in and out of church—who have come under the light of the gospel, but who have never been struck by the Law. (In a later chapter, we will look at how many this may actually be.) They are still asleep in their sins, unaware of their terrible plight because the Law has never awakened them. The power of the Commandments must open their eyes before the light of the gospel can be of benefit. Look at this *sequence* in what Paul writes to the Ephesians: "Therefore He [the Lord] says, 'Awake you who sleep, arise from the dead, and Christ will give you light'" (Ephesians 5:14). There must be an awakening before Jesus Christ gives us light. Dr. Timothy Dwight, former president of Yale University, concluded: "Few, very few, are ever awakened or convinced by the encouragements and promises of the gospel, but almost all by the denunciations of the Law."

> *It isn't the gospel light that will awaken him. How can "Good News" alarm a sinner? No, the Law must strike him.*

I received the following newsletter from someone in New York. This illustrates how the gospel makes little sense without the Law:

> We went to visit [our 96-year-old grandmother] every week and even though she has not received the gospel so freely these past few years, we kept sharing the truth of Jesus with her each time. Mike would play songs about Him. Wendy would talk to her. We would pray for her physical strength and add into the prayer how we wanted God to reveal His Son to Nana.
>
> Then last week, Wendy got the flu, and while she was in bed feeling miserable, she read Ray Comfort's book...which challenges us to share the whole gospel and not sugar-coat it. It talks about using the Law when talking to a sinner to make them see how they have personally broken God's Law and are doomed

without a Savior who paid the price for them. It says in Psalm 19:7 that the "Law of the Lord is perfect, converting the soul." God spoke to Wendy's heart that she needed to share the Law with Nana before Nana could ever see the grace and mercy of God in the cross.

So after committing the day and every detail to God, we went over to visit Nana. She was more alert and less distracted than usual. While Mike was praying, Wendy read her God's Commandments from Exodus 20:1–17 and then asked Nana pointblank, "Nana, have you ever lied? Or stolen anything, even a little thing?" She replied, "I guess so." Wendy shared about God's very real judgments, hell, and heaven, that one day Nana would be standing face to face before God and would have to give an account of her life. Then she read from Isaiah 53:5,6 and told Nana about Jesus and the horror of His cross. Nana looked shocked that someone would have those awful things happen to Him. Wendy shared some of her testimony and then asked Nana if she wanted to ask God to forgive her of her sins. She said yes! And she asked God to forgive her and wash her clean in the blood of Jesus.

This 96-year-old woman didn't know that she was sinning against God until the Law in the hand of the Spirit did its work.

Look at this letter we received from a pastor in Tullahoma, Tennessee:

> I have some great news to share with you. I found out this morning that my father was in the hospital. On the way there to see him, I prayed that God would give me wisdom with the words I was to speak. After being there a few minutes I asked if he had thought any more about our conversation several months ago about

heaven and hell. He replied that he had and said he was ready if it was his time. I pressed him further and then began to use the Law first, going through the Ten Commandments. He began to cry some and admitted he was a Law breaker. I was then privileged to lead him in the prayer of salvation. He looked at me and began crying. I had to leave for a little while and when I came back I told him how glad I was that we had prayed together. He said he was glad too and began to cry again. I am so thankful that at 1:50 p.m. on this day, my dad became a child of God. Thank you, sir, for your obedience in teaching what you do. When my dad saw how utterly sinful he was and that he was without hope and God, he was willing to bow his head and accept Jesus with contrition. He was the first person I have witnessed to using the Law instead of grace first, and I praise God that my dad's salvation is the firstfruits. I used the Law again a few hours later at a store and the guy couldn't say a word. He saw himself a sinner. Again, thank you.

Consider Martin Luther's comments on Romans 7:9 ("I was alive once without the Law, but when the commandment came, sin revived"):

> So it is with the work-righteous and the proud unbelievers. Because they do not know the Law of God, which is directed against them, it is impossible for them to know their sin. Therefore also they are not amenable to instruction. If they would know the Law, they would also know their sin; and sin to which they are now dead would become alive in them.

Jonathan Edwards stated, "The only way we can know whether we are sinning is by knowing His Moral Law." George Whitefield said to his hearers, "First, then, before

121

you can speak peace to your hearts, you must be made to see, made to feel, made to weep over, made to bewail, your actual transgressions against the Law of God." When we preach the whole counsel of God, we merely work with the Holy Spirit to convince people of sin. In *Today's Gospel: Authentic or Synthetic?*, Walter Chantry wrote:

> The absence of God's holy Law from modern preaching is perhaps as responsible as any other factor for the evangelistic impotence of our churches and missions. Only by the light of the Law can the vermin of sin in the heart be exposed. Satan has effectively used a very clever device to silence the Law, which is needed as an instrument to bring perishing men to Christ.

It is imperative that preachers of today learn how to declare the spiritual Law of God; for, until we learn how to wound consciences, we shall have no wounds to bind with gospel bandages.

When we preach the whole counsel of God, we merely work with the Holy Spirit to convince men of sin.

Listen to John MacArthur saying the same thing: "God's grace cannot be faithfully preached to unbelievers until the Law is preached and man's corrupt nature is exposed. It is impossible for a person to fully realize his need for God's grace until he sees how terribly he has failed the standards of God's Law."

According to John Newton, "Ignorance of the nature and design of the Law is at the bottom of most religious mistakes." Charles Spurgeon stated, "I do not believe that any man can preach the gospel who does not preach the Law." Then he warns, "Lower the Law and you dim the light by which man perceives his guilt; this is a very serious loss to the sinner rather than a gain; for it lessens the likelihood of his conviction and conversion. I say you have deprived the gospel of its ablest auxiliary [its most powerful weapon] when you have set aside the Law. You have taken away from it the schoolmaster that is to bring men to Christ ...*They will never accept grace till they tremble before a just and holy Law.* Therefore the Law serves a most necessary purpose, and it must not be removed from its place."

Listen to the wisdom of great men of God from ages past:

John Wesley: "It remains only to show...the uses of the Law. And the first use of it, without question, is to convince the world of sin. By this is the sinner discovered to himself. All his fig-leaves are torn away, and he sees that he is 'wretched and poor and miserable, blind and naked.' The Law flashes conviction on every side. He feels himself a mere sinner. He has nothing to pay. His 'mouth is stopped' and he stands 'guilty before God.' To slay the sinner is then the first use of the Law, to destroy the life and strength wherein he trusts and convince him that he is dead while he lives; not only under the sentence of death, but actually dead to God, void of all spiritual life, dead in trespasses and sins."

Charles Spurgeon: "The Law cuts into the core of the evil, it reveals the seat of the malady, and informs us that the leprosy lies deep within."

John Bunyan: "The man who does not know the nature of the Law, cannot know the nature of sin."

Martin Luther: "The first duty of the Gospel preacher is to declare God's Law and show the nature of sin...We would not see nor realize it (what a distressing and horrible fall in which we lie), if it were not for the Law, and we would have to remain forever lost, if we were not again helped out of it through Christ. Therefore the Law and the Gospel are given to the end that we may learn to know both how guilty we are and to what we should again return."

J. I. Packer: "Unless we see our shortcomings in the light of the Law and holiness of God, we do not see them as sin at all."

John Wesley: "He cries out, O what love have I to thy Law! All the day long is my study in it. He sees daily, in that divine mirror, more and more of his own sinfulness. He sees more and more clearly, that he is fullness a sinner in all things—that neither his heart nor his ways are right before God, and that every moment sends him to Christ. Therefore I cannot spare the Law one moment, no more than I can spare Christ, seeing I now want it as much to keep me to Christ, as I ever wanted it to bring me to Him. Otherwise this 'evil heart of unbelief' would immediately 'depart from the living God.' Indeed each is continually sending me to the other—the Law to Christ, and Christ to the Law." —*KC*

Look at how the Law did its part in bringing Robert Flockhart, one of Spurgeon's favorite preachers, to the cross:

> I consider the language of the apostle in Romans 7:9 not inapplicable to my situation at that time, "but when the commandment came, sin revived, and I died." Sin, that had been asleep before, came like a giant upon me. I saw myself in the mirror of God's Law. That Law was spiritual and extended to the thoughts and intents of my heart. Dreadful and blasphemous thoughts, like sparks out of a chimney, now came out of my heart. I was afraid to open my Bible or even to look up, for fear the Lord would send a thunderbolt out of heaven to crush me.

What a translation from darkness to light, from the kingdom of darkness to the kingdom of God's dear Son! My guilt removed and my pardon sealed, peace flowed like a river into my soul (*The Street Preacher*, pp. 77,81).

Perhaps modern evangelism's reticence to preach what produces fear is simply due to concern about the reaction of sinners. Some may worry that the message may be aligned with what is commonly called "hell-fire" preaching. Yet there is a vast difference between the use of the Law and hell-fire preaching. Understandably, the thought of the existence of hell, without the use of the Law to justify its existence, is unreasonable to a sinner's mind. How could a God of love create a place of eternal torment? Imagine if the police suddenly burst into your home, thrust you into prison, and angrily shouted, "You are going away for a long time!" Such conduct would undoubtedly leave you bewildered and angry. What they have done is *unreasonable*.

However, if the law burst into your home and instead told you specifically why you were in trouble by saying, "We have discovered 10,000 marijuana plants growing in your backyard. You are going away for a long time!" at least you would understand why you are in trouble. Knowledge of the law you transgressed furnished you with understanding. It makes judgment *reasonable*.

Hell-fire preaching without use of the Law to show the sinner *why* God is angry with him will more than likely leave him bewildered and angry—for what he considers unreasonable punishment. However, when we use the Law lawfully, it appeals to the "reason" of sinners. Paul *reasoned* with Felix about judgment to come and his sins, to the point where the governor "was afraid" (Acts 24:25). Hell became reasonable. No doubt the "righteousness" Paul spoke of was the righteousness which is of the Law, and the result was that the fear of God fell upon the heart of his hearer.

Those who come to the Savior with such knowledge are not strangers to fear, even after the cross. They tremble at the cost of their redemption. They gaze with fear-filled hearts at the grizzly sight of Calvary's cross. They work out their own salvation with "fear and trembling" because they were not redeemed "with silver and gold, but with the precious blood of Christ."

In his wonderful book *Fresh Wind, Fresh Fire*, Jim Cymbala, rightly frustrated by the lukewarm contemporary Church, says of the disciples:

> Once they were empowered on the Day of Pentecost, however, they became the church victorious, the church militant. With the gracious manifestation of God's Spirit in the Upper Room, the disciples encountered their first audience. Peter, the biggest failure of them all, became the preacher that day. It was no homiletical masterpiece, to be sure. But people were deeply convicted—"cut to the heart," according to Acts 2:37 —by his anointed words. Three thousand were gathered into the church that day (p. 92).

The inference is that the key was the empowerment of the Holy Spirit. This is true. However, we have the same Holy Spirit nowadays, and we rarely see such a harvest of souls. Why not? Simply because Peter properly prepared the ground upon which he was sowing. His audience was composed of "devout men" who were gathered at Pentecost to celebrate the giving of God's Law on Mount Sinai.

Even though these were godly Jews, Peter told them that they were "lawless"—that they had violated God's Law by murdering Jesus (Acts 2:23). He drove home that fact by saying, "Therefore let all the house of Israel know assuredly that God has made this Jesus, *whom you crucified,* both Lord and Christ" (Acts 2:36, emphasis added). It was then that they saw that their sin was personal. They were "cut to the heart" and cried out for help. Only after the Law convicted them of their sinfulness did Peter offer them grace (v. 38).

This was also the case with Nicodemus and Nathanael. Nicodemus was a leader of the Jews whom Jesus called a "teacher of Israel" (John 3:10). He was therefore thoroughly versed in God's Law. He also had a humble heart. Here was a leader of the Jews acknowledging the deity of the Son of God (John 3:2). The Law was a schoolmaster to bring this humble, godly Jew to Christ.

We have the same Holy Spirit nowadays, and we rarely see such a harvest of souls. Why not?

According to John 1:47, Jesus said that Nathanael was an Israelite (brought up under the Law) in whom there was "no deceit" (he didn't twist the Law as the Pharisees did; he no doubt read "the way of God in truth"). The Law also served as a schoolmaster to bring this godly Jew to the Savior.

THE BADGE OF AUTHORITY

13

America has chosen to live in moral darkness. Its Constitution has replaced Holy Scripture as the point of moral reference. The writings of men have become sacred. Contemporary America is no different than the Pharisees of Christ's time, whose decrees made the Word of God void.

Take, for instance, pornography. Why should our government tolerate such moral perversion? To them, the answer is clear from the writings of our forefathers—it is a "constitutional right" to produce unclean literature, even if it is morally offensive. However, ask a man who advocates pornographic literature if *child* porn is legitimate, and he will usually draw his moral line. Ask him then at what age "immoral" child porn crosses the divide and becomes "morally acceptable." You will find, with a little digging, that the dividing line is the line of *personal pleasure*. He doesn't gain pleasure from a 13-year-old child, but does from a 17-year-old young woman. His love for sin clouds his moral judgment.

The Constitution of the United States is being used for something it was never intended. When a legal document is employed as a moral beacon, we end up with morally blind legislators leading a morally blind nation. Both fall into a dirty ditch. However, the argument for pornography is concluded with one statement from Holy Scripture: "Whoever looks at a woman to lust for her has already committed adultery with her in his heart" (Matthew 5:28). Case closed.

When we specifically point to the Scriptures as an ethical beacon, we must make it clear to those who will listen that our express reference is the Moral Law of God. There is great reason for this. In 1989, when I first came to the United States, I was preaching in the open air at Venice Beach, California. Unbeknown to me at that time, the police there wore shorts and rode around on bicycles.

When I stood on a soapbox and began to speak on the edge of the wide sidewalk, a crowd of about 80 people gathered around to listen. Suddenly, a man in shorts stood right in front of me and told me to stop. When I ignored him, he became very indignant and told me once again to stop. I asked, "Are you a police officer?" He then became angry and said through gritted teeth, "If you don't stop right now, I will arrest you!"

It was then that I noticed a badge on his belt, which told me he *was* an officer of the law. Suddenly, his words carried a great deal of authority! I was elevated above him, and his badge was out of my sight, so I had no respect for him other than what I would give an ordinary civilian.

Those who are representatives of the living God, yet who don't point to the Law as the core of their authority, will not gain due consideration from the world. Jesus stood before the multitudes as One who was a representative of the Law of God. The Bible says the Messiah would bring justice to the earth and that the "coastlands will wait for His law" (Isaiah 42:4). He repeatedly referred to the Law as the point of His authority, saying, "I did not come to destroy [the Law] but to fulfill," "One jot or one tittle will by no means pass from the Law," "This is the Law and the Prophets," "Have you not read in the Law...?" "It is easier for heaven and earth to pass away than for one tittle of the Law to fail" (Matthew 5:17,18; 7:12; Luke 16:17).

Abortion is wrong. Adultery is wrong. Pornography is wrong. We can shout our moral convictions from the highest housetops, but the world will not listen.* It exalts itself above the claims of the Christian faith. It has no incentive to open its heart to what we have to say.

> * While I was on an airplane recently, a flight attendant asked me if it was true that I was very religious. After telling her about my love for Jesus, she smugly replied, "Well, we all have our own opinions, right?" True, we each have only our own opinion. That is why we must not assert just a personal opinion, but the true, authoritative Word of God. When a man hears from the Supreme Judge of his soul that what he is doing is wrong, he realizes the foolishness of his rebellion. —KC

Why did I suddenly take notice of the man who was telling me to stop? *It was his badge that caused me to take notice.* His badge said that if I didn't heed his words there would be coming judgment. To tell the world that it's wrong to kill, to steal, to commit adultery, without reference to future punishment, is to point an unloaded cannon.

Some may listen because morality does have positive influences. Theft can ravage a society. Adultery can ruin families. Lying can shatter friendships. In that context morality makes sense. However, when we tell the world to repent because God has "appointed a day on which He will judge the world in righteousness" (Acts 17:31), they will have an inducement to obey the gospel. It will begin to dawn on them that their own eternal welfare is at stake.

Again, for the Church to neglect to point to the Law of God is to hide the badge of our authority from the world. Understandably, sinners will disregard what we have to say. The gospel we preach is only there because God stands by the holiness of the Law. If Eternal Law didn't exist, then there would have been no need for a sacrifice. The Law demands retribution. It was the divine fire of God's Law that fell on the sacrifice of Calvary.

If the world *knew* that there is an Eternal Law they must face, that the Law necessitates death and hell for transgression, then they would seriously consider the claims of the gospel. If they understood that the long arm of the Law will reach right down into the heart of humanity, they would repent. If they knew that Almighty God is angry at the wicked every day, that His wrath abides on them, they would flee to the Savior.

It was in the darkness of the Law that Paul saw the light of the glorious gospel.

Let me put it another way. Each of the Ten Commandments is of itself a "key." However, these are not keys that *release*; instead, they are keys that lock the sinner in the holding cell of sin and death. Paul spoke of being "kept under guard" by the Law. He was left without hope, condemned, waiting for capital punishment from the hand of the Law he had so blatantly violated.

When speaking of God's Law, Charles Spurgeon said, "Having thus removed the mask and shown the desperate case of the sinner, the relentless Law causes the offense to abound yet more by bringing home the sentence of condemnation. It mounts the judgment seat, puts on the black cap and pronounces the sentence of death. With a harsh unpitying voice it solemnly thunders forth the words 'condemned already!'"

It was in the darkness of the Law that Paul saw the light of the glorious gospel. The grace of God pointed him to another door—the Door of the Savior. He could leave the cell because his fine had been paid in full by the shed blood of the spotless Lamb of God. It was the Law that showed Paul that he was unable to save himself. He knew that salvation was an act of mercy—that his deliverance from death was the result of God's grace, not something in his own character that drew mercy toward him.

> The Law didn't help me, it just left me helpless. It didn't make me a good person, it made me realize that I'm not. The Law is the mirror that shows you and me that we're in trouble with God and cannot help ourselves; we must rely completely upon Jesus to save us. I thank God for the Law. Without it, I'd still be living in a dream world, thinking I was going to heaven when, in reality, I was on my way to hell! —KC

This principle was clearly illustrated as I was preaching open-air in the Third Street Promenade of Santa Monica, California, where I had a permit to speak. I had been taking a team there each Friday night for more than two years, and only once before had I seen such antagonism toward the gospel. There was the usual bitter animosity from the products of modern evangelism. One man, betraying his "Christian" background, started preaching about his hamster dying for the sins of the world, and if only we would give our hearts to him, we would find peace and joy. When a professing atheist named James began to mock the things of God by yelling "Praise Jesus" among other things, my suspicions were confirmed when he admitted that he had once given his heart to Christ. A sweet teenage girl, a Mormon, kept shouting that I was Satan, and tried to shock me by baring her breasts (I looked the other way). Others were spitting and using language that would make your hair curl tighter than a pig's tail. Among a number of others, three teenage girls came to the "heckler's" microphone and said that they were witches. A few years ago I would have doubted what they said, but I believed their testimony.

For many years I have used a mannequin (a dummy) called Lazarus, who would quietly lie under a sheet as a crowd-getter. People would often stop and ask, "What have you got *that* there for?" To which I would reply, "It's to get people to stop and ask, 'What have you got *that* there for?' It works, doesn't it?"[7]

On this particular night, Lazarus received his share of persecution. One young man began doing lewd acts on him, much to the delight of the crowd. While I was speaking, another youth burst into the crowd, rushed up to Lazarus, and stomped on his head. It was such a violent act that Lazarus' plastic face actually burst. I jumped off my soapbox, grabbed the youth by his shirt, and said, "That dummy cost me a lot of money. Give me $80 right now or you are in big trouble." I looked him in the eyes and said, "You are under citizen's arrest for willful damage of my property. I'm calling the police."

He looked scared and said, "You can have everything I have." He immediately handed me a fistful of dollars. I passed it to a friend, who counted it and said that there was only $28. I told the youth that wasn't enough and I wanted the full $80. He protested that he didn't have any more cash.

By this time a large crowd had gathered, so (still holding the youth by the shirt) I said, "Just as I am holding this man because he has transgressed the law, so God has placed you in a holding cell for transgression of *His* Law. The sentence for your crimes against God is death."

I then went through the Law into grace and said, "God is rich in mercy and sent His Son to pay the fine for you." I preached the cross, faith, and repentance...still holding the young man tightly by his shirt. I told the crowd that because Jesus paid the fine in full for us on the cross, God can extend His mercy toward us. We are free to go.

Then I turned to the youth, stuffed the money in his hand, and said, "Here's your money back. Neither am I going to call the police. You are free to go."

It was such a clear illustration of God's mercy. The young man's guilt was evident (he had been caught in the act). He couldn't make atonement. He deserved nothing but judgment, but instead received mercy. His mouth dropped open in unbelief.

SIN'S PLEASURE

Someone once called me and asked for my advice about a publication he wanted to produce. It was to help men who were addicted to pornography. He was going to write his experience in tract form, relating how pornography had ruined him. The vice produced guilt, ruined his marriage, and made him a slave to his passions. His thought was that the negative fruit of the sin would steer men away from it. His philosophy sounds good, but it rarely works. If it did, we wouldn't have so many people smoking cigarettes, abusing drugs, gambling, and drinking alcohol. The evidence that smoking results in a slow and painful death doesn't deter smokers. Drug abuse kills. Gambling destroys homes and lives. Cities with legalized gambling have been found to have higher rates of crime, suicide, bankruptcy, and other social ills; yet, people gamble. Multitudes still blindly dive into a sea of poison called alcohol, despite the mass of dead bodies piled on the shore.

People know the consequences of a sinful lifestyle, but the immediate pleasure far outweighs the fear of long-term negative consequences. Sinful man will not give up his darling lust unless he has a good reason to. Hell is a good reason.

In speaking with my father about reasons why we should obey God, he said that hell definitely grabs his attention, and that he didn't want to go there because he has a very low tolerance for pain. —KC

In the next chapter, we'll look at how the Ten Commandments can be used effectively in personal witnessing.

14

DON'T LEAVE
ME LIKE THIS!

I was in Baltimore without a meeting on a Sunday night, so I decided to change my plane ticket to go home early. When I called, the reservation agent gave the name of the airline, told me her name was Fran, and asked how she could be of help to me. I explained my situation, and made her laugh a little to a point where I had the liberty to ask about her spiritual life. I said, "Fran, are you a Christian?" She answered, "No. I don't accept the virgin birth." I explained to her that that wasn't the issue with her at the moment, but that her big problem was the Ten Commandments. I asked, "Have you ever told a lie?" She said she had. She also admitted that she had stolen. When I explained that Jesus said that lust was the same as adultery in God's sight, and asked her if she had lusted, she said, "Of course."

I said, "Fran, by your own admission, you are a lying, thieving, adulterer-at-heart. You have to face God on Judgment Day, *and we have looked at only three of the Ten Commandments.*" I then said, "I would like a window seat if possible." She didn't appreciate the change of subject, and said, *"Don't leave me like this!"* Gently, I said, "What's wrong, Fran, don't you like being left with your conscience?" I went on to reason with her about her salvation, about Judgment Day, then the cross.

We shouldn't be afraid to make the sinner tremble. Which is worse: a little trembling because of guilt, or eternity in the lake of fire? Men like Whitefield and others preached until the Law "stopped the mouth" and sinners hung their heads in shame. They weren't afraid to use the terrors of the Law to drive men to the cross. A resurrected and accusing conscience is the first evidence of the beginnings of the work of the Holy Spirit. It is a great mistake to muffle its voice with talk of God's forgiveness before it has a chance to do its precious work.

Fran didn't get angry at me. I wasn't judging her. She was the one who admitted her sins. Besides, what could she say: "I thought lying, stealing, etc., were right"? She couldn't *begin* to justify her sins in light of her quickened conscience. It is because of the ally of the "work of the Law" that we can gently say "hard" things to sinners.

> A resurrected and accusing conscience is the first evidence of the beginnings of the work of the Holy Spirit.

It is interesting to note that the conscience doesn't join in with the pleasures of sin. The unregenerate person loves sin with all of his heart, mind, soul, and strength. However, the judge in the courtroom of the mind stands aloof and makes an impartial judgment. It is the "conscience also bearing witness, . . . their thoughts accusing or else excusing them" (Romans 2:15). The judge gives a *guilty* or *not guilty* verdict of what is evidenced before it.

In parts of Africa during the drought season, antelope are drawn by thirst to pools of muddy water. Without drink they will die of dehydration. Hidden in the foul waters lie hungry and vicious crocodiles. The only thing visible in the water, to the discerning, is the naked eye of the monster as it watches the antelope's every movement.

Desire so consumes the animal that he slowly ventures to the water's edge, and completely lets down his God-given guard as he drinks in the life-giving liquid. Instinct warns him of the danger, but his unquenchable thirst drives him to the water. Suddenly, great jaws open and amid the splashing of water, the animal is pulled to a terrifying death.

The sinner is drawn to the muddy pool of iniquity by his uncontrollable thirst for sin. The cries of his God-given conscience are muffled at the sight of what lies before him. Suddenly, death seizes upon him in an instant and he is gone forever, swallowed by the jaws of everlasting hell.

The Law reveals the crocodile *before* it attacks. As the sinner drinks in the waters of sin, he suddenly sees sin's terrible form as it lies hidden in the pool. This is what Paul is speaking about in Romans 7:8–12. The Law showed him the appetite in the eye of the beast, causing him to quickly draw back from the pool of iniquity.

So Long, Pal!

We regularly receive calls on our 800 number from dyslexic people who misdial the number they are calling. Very early one morning a deep-voiced gentleman phoned, thinking he was calling a company that sells farm supplies. I told him that he had transposed the last two digits, then said to make sure he read his Bible. He said he wouldn't, because he was an atheist. For the next few minutes I reasoned with him about the necessity of having a maker for everything that was made. It was a spirited fight, but it was merely swordplay. The moment would come when I would have to get my point across, to go for the kill. I took the Commandments in hand and lunged toward the heart: "Do you think you have kept the Ten Commandments?" He said he thought he had. "Have you ever told a lie?" He had, but would not hold still for a second and admit that he was a liar. He jumped back and forth, insisting that someone who told lies was "human," just told "fibs," or was "weak, like everyone else."

When I pressed the point, he suddenly spat out, "Okay, I'm a liar!" We touched on two other Commandments which he admitted to transgressing, the existence of his conscience, and the fact of Judgment Day. Suddenly, his references to evolution, other people's sins, and hypocrisy in the Church were no longer the issue. He was mortally wounded...cut to the heart. He staggered backward and protested, "I'm a good person!" I thrust back, "No, you're not. You're a lying thief!" The pain was too much for him. He said, *So long, pal!* and hung up in my ear.

The Law showed him the appetite in the eye of the beast, causing him to quickly draw back from the pool of iniquity.

I sat by the phone and wished that he had stayed in the fight for another minute. I would have told him that he was just adding self-righteousness to his sin. I would also have liked to tell him to study Matthew 24 and Luke 21, which would prove to him that the Bible is the Word of the Creator. Then I prayed that God's hand would be upon him.

About ten seconds later, the phone rang again. When I picked it up, I heard a deep-voiced and mystified man mumble, "What's going on? How did I get you again? I tried to call this number, and instead I get one that makes my blood hot!"

Hot blood means that life is present. He was no longer a

cold-blooded atheist. *I was beside myself with joy.* I told him to read Matthew 24 and Luke 21. Then I gave him my name and said he could call our 800 number anytime. When he kept mumbling, "Why did I call you again?" I could think of only two alternatives. Either he was a dummy and had called the wrong number again, or God's hand was upon him. I told him that it was because God's hand was upon him. He didn't argue about that, and this time our parting was more congenial.

RIGHT NUMBER

It was a Friday afternoon. The phone rang, and when I answered it I heard, "Is this Direct Imports?" I said it wasn't and asked what number the man wanted. He gave our number so I said, "Well, that is our number, but before you go, *make sure you read your Bible.*" He became quiet, then asked, "Why's that?" I said so that he could find how to secure his eternal destiny and added, "There's nothing more important than that, is there?" He said, "Yi, yi, yi…I'd better sit down for this!" I asked, "Are you Jewish?" When he said he was, I told him that I was also Jewish and remarked, "Remember, you've got to face the Ten Commandments on Judgment Day."

His reply was interesting: "I have done research, specifically on the adultery one, and I've come to the conclusion that you can fool around with a woman as long as she's not married." I said, "If you as much as look with lust, the Bible says that you commit adultery in your heart. Have you ever told a lie?" He had. I asked if he had stolen; he had. So I gently told him that he was, by his own admission, a lying, thieving adulterer, and that's why he needed the Savior, Jesus Christ—to save him from God's anger. I told him to read his Bible and seek God for the salvation of his soul. I also invited him to call my number anytime if he wanted to talk in the future. His voice sounded quite depressed as he said, "Thank you very much for talking to me." I think I ruined his weekend.

In the following chapter we're going to look closely at a very important question: What is it that sparks a burning flame of passion for the lost in the heart of a believer?

15

TAKE TWO TABLETS AND CALL ME WHEN YOU'RE MOURNING

Why are there so few front-line soldiers within the Body of Christ? There are many who say that they love God, read the Word, pray, and praise God with a passion, but there are so few who have what Spurgeon referred to as a deep "tenderness." These are the ones who carry an anguish of soul for the fate of the ungodly. They break out of their complacency and seek by any means to save that which is lost. The love of Christ "compels" them (2 Corinthians 5:14). The Greek word used denotes that His love arrests them, preoccupies and presses them to reach out to the lost. These are the ones of whom Jesus said there was a great and tragic lack (Matthew 9:37,38), commanding us to pray that God would give us more. They take off their jackets of condescension, put on the armor of light, and go to battle.

For years I couldn't discover what it was that forged these rare and hardy souls. Were these merely diamonds that sparkled more than others because of a God-given temperament? Were these people born fearless by nature and their bold and zealous witness came naturally to them, out-sparkling others who lacked such a virtue? No, some of the most zealous and bold witnesses of Christ I have known have been of a quiet or even a shy disposition.

One night in late 1994, I found the answer. A friend, Pastor Mike Smalley, and I were at the home of Winkie and Faye Pratney deep in the heart of Texas. Winkie is a fellow New Zealander, so it was something special for us to get together for dinner—it called for steak.

Winkie went outside to put the steaks on a barbecue, but a few minutes later reluctantly brought them back inside when the barbie ran out of propane gas. As he cooked them inside, he said something about them not being as tender as they would have been if he had cooked them on the intense heat of the barbecue.

After a few minutes, the entire house filled with smoke from his cooking; but it was well worth it—the steaks melted in the mouth. Besides, the fans in the house soon cleared the air.

When I remarked about the tenderness of my steak, Winkie shared his secret. He explained that the way to keep a steak tender is to sear it on both sides for forty seconds on a very hot hotplate. That seals the juices in the steak, then you cook it slowly until it is done.

About 3:00 a.m. the following morning, it dawned on me about what produces the much-desired tenderhearted Christian. When a sinner comes under the intense heat of the Law of God, it has the effect of sealing within him a tender heart. This is how it happens: As the spirituality of the Law bears down on him, it shows him the exceeding sinfulness of his heart. It reveals to him that the very core of his nature is vile, that his lust is adultery, that hatred is murder, that he is a liar, a thief, and a rebel—a selfish and ungrateful sinner.

He begins to see that he has loved what is abhorrent to his Creator. The Law shows him that even his so-called "good" works are tainted by a self-centered motive. This knowledge coupled with the fact that he has *greatly* angered God by transgressing His Law, and that hell is his just dessert, is the "heat" that seals in the tenderness of soul.

When grace is revealed, it is embraced as a man dying of thirst embraces a jug of water. The experience of the searing heat of the Law bringing him to the point of death, yet being freely given the waters of life, forever secures the virtue of unspeakable gratitude. And that makes him a laborer for life. The Law gives him understanding that in the gospel he is forgiven much, so he loves much—vertically and therefore horizontally.

Such tenderness is difficult to cultivate in someone who already possesses knowledge of God's grace in Christ. His realization of God's goodness deprives him of the fear of wrath. Only those who can sing "and grace my fears relieved" see grace as being truly amazing. This is why I believe it is a mistake to tell a guilty unregenerate sinner "God loves you." Such knowledge doesn't allow fear to enter his heart. That deprives him of a depth of gratitude he would otherwise have if fear had been allowed to do its work.

Only those who can sing "and grace my fears relieved" see grace as being truly amazing.

This is why the enlightened witness of Christ is not afraid to gently put on the heat when speaking with sinners. He knows that when the smoke of the wrath of the Law condemns the prisoner before him, it is actually preparing his heart for a pardon that will be welcomed *because of the fear gripping the prisoner's heart.* The Christian knows that the tears that fear produces will be wiped away by the gentle hand of God's grace. He knows that that hand will not be fully appreciated if the Law is not allowed to do its most necessary work. It is the Law of God that exposes sin, and when sin is viewed under the penetrating light of the Law, as we have seen, it makes grace "abound." The Greek word used to explain this in Romans 5:20 is *hyperperisseuo,* which means to "superabound."

If I were a physician and I knew you had a terrible disease, I would be unwise to give you a cure without first carefully explaining to you that you had the disease. However, I wouldn't merely tell you that you had the disease; I would actually let fear work for your good. I would use it to cause you to *want* to take the cure. As I showed you x-rays, I would watch beads of sweat drip from your brow and say to myself, "Good, he's beginning to see the seriousness of his disease." The fear will not only cause you to embrace the cure, it will (when the cure is received) give you tremendous appreciation for me as your doctor for providing the cure.

One day I determined to witness to a very dear friend of the family who had stopped by for a visit. Her name is Kristy and she is 13 years old. We began talking about spiritual things in a casual conversation. I told her I wanted to read her something, and I read her a portion of Revelation 20 about Judgment Day. I reasoned with her about God's love for justice and that God must punish sin wherever it is found. We read other passages about false believers and where they would spend eternity. She was frightened for them and we talked about the mirror of the Law to see if we are ourselves are safe on Judgment Day. When we went through the Commandments, she felt guilty and began to confess secret sins of theft, lying, hatred, etc. I had her read from the Scriptures about the destiny of liars, thieves, blasphemers, slanderers, and idolaters, all of which she admittedly was. She concluded that she'd be guilty on the Day of Judgment and would therefore go to hell for eternity. She was visibly upset and concerned. I could see tears begin to form as she held her head low. To see her realize her hellbound destiny broke my heart, but thrilled it as well, because I knew that this girl was about to hear the best news of her life. Fear and guilt produced by her conscience had thoroughly gripped her heart; the soil was now ready for the seed of the gospel.

I asked Kristy if she knew what God had done so she wouldn't have to go to hell. She didn't know, although she mumbled the word, "Forgiveness?"

I told her about Jesus' suffering death as payment for her sins. She broke the Law, and Jesus paid her fine. I read her Isaiah 53:5,6 and showed her the way of salvation through repentance and faith in Jesus. I asked her if she'd ever been born again. She hadn't but said she wanted that new heart promised in the Scriptures because she feared that even if God forgave her of her sins, she might sin again. What a wonderful attitude! To cower at the thought of offending God even one more time—oh, beautiful Spirit of God, please sustain that holy fear in me! "The fear of the Lord is the beginning of wisdom." Because of her fear of the Lord, I had the privilege of detailing the wonders of God's faithfulness to create in her a new heart with new desires, and His promise to forgive and cleanse her of all unrighteousness (1 John 1:9).

Kristy silently prayed for forgiveness and a new heart of obedience. Then I prayed for her protection, blessing, and her new life in Christ. When I asked her how she felt, her face broke into a huge smile as she said, "Much better." She gave me a hug and thanked me for talking with her. I bought her a teen Bible and encouraged her to read it every day. She was very excited.

Later my wife, Chelsea, said that Kristy was so grateful to finally understand why Jesus died on the cross for her. Kristy said that it had never made sense to her before—not even when she went forward to "accept Jesus" in church. The day she responded at the altar, she simply raised her hand at the invitation to "accept Jesus into your heart and have your sins forgiven so you'll go to heaven." Who wouldn't accept that? The problem was that she had no real knowledge of her sin, so she couldn't repent or understand the cross. But when the Law revealed her exceedingly sinful heart, she ran into the arms of Jesus for forgiveness and a new heart. And to think that I once thought the Law was outdated and useless! Praise God for continuing to teach me! —KC

A great preacher once asked a well-known actor how it was that when performers present a story they often bring the audience to tears, yet rarely do ministers move a congregation to such a degree. The actor responded that they portray fiction as if it were a reality, while ministers of the gospel too often portray reality as if it were fiction.

If we really believed souls were going to hell, we would preach with overwhelming passion. Our hearts would groan in constant prayer. We would run to sinners with solemn words of warning, take hold of them and beseech them to turn from sin. Instead, we lack any real sense of urgency. We are afraid to speak frankly with sinners about their personal sins. We think that searing them under the heat of the Law will do harm rather than good. But consider how

Jesus spoke with the woman at the well in John chapter 4. He applied the heat of the Law to her (v. 18) and spoke of her *personal* transgressions—and what was the result? She became an immediate laborer (vv. 28,29).[8]

I received the following letter about one of my books, which shows the power of the Law to bring a thirst for righteousness:

> This friend of mine has always told me for the last eight years whenever the opportunity popped up, that the Law was finished with and that the Ten Commandments were basically useless. Of course, I tried to gently suggest that the knowledge of sin could not come by any other way than the Law, but this was always smothered in a sugary reference to love and grace...so I kept quiet.
>
> But I stuck my neck out last week and gave the book to this friend, and the next day he handed it back to me. He was crying and shaking with emotion. He could hardly speak. He said, "I've just been born again!" What really happened, I think, was the full impact of the power of God's Law had struck him and wounded him, showing him clearly how bad his sin really was. He was in quite a state for several days after that, and kept breaking out into praise to God.

It was the two tablets of the Law that caused the mourning in his heart.

SEVEN SCARED SINNERS

Late in 1994, I arrived in Baton Rouge to do a series of meetings. A young man named Jeff picked me up and told me of the plan he had for me to speak open-air at a fake funeral.

After a short sleep in my hotel I was picked up, briefed

the pallbearers, the corpse, and the crowd as to the do's and don'ts of an open-air setting, then we drove to the site of the preaching.

When we pulled into the parking lot of a Wal-Mart I thought we were going to buy something, but it was actually the location Jeff had chosen for us. After about five minutes of preaching, one of the security guards approached me and said I could speak for another five minutes, then I had to stop. I was thankful for the extra time, and afterwards mentioned this to the local pastor who had come with us. He smiled and said, "When you started, I told the security guard, 'See all those people around the preacher? They go to my church and we all shop at Wal-Mart.'"

After that, we drove to an area near the local university campus and set up the funeral once again. This time Jeff had decided he would give my voice a break by preaching himself. Just as we were organizing the pallbearers, a siren shrieked behind me. I turned to see a traffic officer on a motorcycle angrily waving over a van full of teenagers. As the van pulled to the side of the road the police officer jumped off his bike, ran to the van, opened the door, and cursed the driver. He then grabbed him, violently pulled him out of his seat, and thrust him against the vehicle. The officer then gave him a body search, once again using obscenities as he did so. The scared youth didn't resist as he was frisked and yelled at.

From what I could gather, the officer had waved the van over and they had failed to stop. Some of the passengers in the van had thought the incident funny, which had caused the officer to boil over. Here was a wrath-filled, slightly out-of-control officer of the law, "God's minister, an avenger to execute wrath on him who practices evil" (Romans 13:4). We decided that it wouldn't be wise to preach there with the law so upset, so we moved to the entrance of a bar about 30 yards across the parking lot. While Jeff preached, semi-drunken teenagers came out of the bar and mocked him. It was a replay of what I had just seen in the natural realm. These teens were refusing to listen to the Law, and they were storing up wrath that would be revealed on the Day of Wrath. The Day would come when an angry Law would pull them from the seat of the scornful, and from that there would be no escape.

After about five minutes, the manager came out and stopped Jeff from preaching (the local church members didn't patronize his bar).

As we wandered back to the van, we passed the youths the officer had stopped. I went over to the group and asked what had happened. The driver was obviously still upset and told me that he had driven through a stop sign, had his lights out, and had failed to stop when the officer first waved him over. His six friends who were with him were also shaken by what had taken place. I couldn't help but sympathize a little with the driver and shared how I thought the officer had clearly lost control of himself. He agreed.

I wanted to witness to them, but felt I lacked the right approach. They were like a distressed child who had just grazed his leg, and I had arrived to put salt in the wound. I was sure that if I mentioned sin, righteousness, and judgment at that point I would be told in no uncertain and colorful terms to depart from the area. Reluctantly, I simply said I would see them later and walked back to our group.

As I stood there, someone asked if I had witnessed to them. I said I hadn't. I told the person that I didn't know how to approach the subject and that I needed a little time to get some thoughts together.

A moment later, I walked back to them determined to

say something about their eternal salvation, even if I did get abused. Suddenly, I remembered that I had put about ten one-dollar bills in my wallet to give away at the open-air, something I often do to illustrate a number of points.[9] When I asked how much the fine would be, the driver looked up and said, "About $200." I took my wallet out, pulled out the handful of bills and said, "This isn't much, but I would like to give this toward the fine." As I referred to the money, I looked down at it in amazement. Clearly visible in the middle of the wad of bills was a ten-dollar bill, making it look like far more than it was. *It looked like a fortune!*

> "Now you know you have transgressed the Divine Law. If civil law scared you, wait until you face God on Judgment Day."

Different teens in the group said, "Wow...you can't do that...that's really nice of you...you don't even know us." The driver graciously declined the money, but the offer struck a chord in their hearts. They could see that I really cared about them and the suggestion had given me license to speak to them about their salvation. I said, "I'm a preacher. Here is a gift for each of you." I then handed each of them a penny with the Ten Commandments pressed onto it, and asked if they had kept the Law. When I asked if they had lied, stolen, lusted, etc., every one of them admitted that they had broken the Commandments.

Then I turned to the driver and asked him if he was scared when the law pulled him from his vehicle. He said he was terrified. I then said, "Tonight you transgressed civil law, but now you know that you have also transgressed the Divine Law. If civil law scared you, wait until you face God on Judgment Day—it is a fearful thing to fall into the hands of the living God." I explained the gospel, asked if they had

Bibles, and told them to dust them off and read the Gospel of John. I then shook their hands, thanked them for listening, and left them in the hands of a faithful Creator.

While I had been speaking, the driver was peeling masking tape from around his ankles. He had strapped sealed plastic bags of whiskey under his socks—something the law hadn't found when he was frisked. God only knows what may have happened that night if the driver had downed the whiskey and driven home with six drunken friends in his van.

The officer of the law missed that hidden offense, but God's Law won't miss a thing.

Both the civil and the Divine Law did a deep work in some young hearts that night. It was my prayer that seven "steaks" were seared to a crisp, and that some day seven tenderhearted and faithful laborers would enter the harvest fields and gladly toil for their Master.

By the way, Winkie Pratney's talents were not confined to cooking steak. The man is not only an excellent Bible teacher and author, but a brilliant ping-pong player as well, as I found out two days later. I also discovered that his style of demonstrative play was reminiscent of a pregnant woman in the latter stages of labor. Despite the sweat, groans, and screams when the man missed a shot, I learned that he was extremely talented. He played with the grace of a master. His speed, his genius, his reflexes, his dazzling shots were executed with astounding agility. Only occasionally does one get to witness such incredible brilliance.

I beat him.

The next chapter is the one that ignited a roaring fire of revival within my own heart, and moved me to seek and save the lost *now*! —KC

16

AN ANGRY GOD

I f our theology leaves out the Law and thus the necessity of the Holy Spirit's conviction of sin, we will see nothing wrong with leaving a sinner with false peace. Remember that in Jeremiah 8:11 God said of the prophets and priests of Israel:

> They have healed the hurt of the daughter of My people slightly, saying, "Peace, peace!" when there is no peace.

This is how to give false peace to a sinner. Simply ask, "Do you have assurance that you will go to heaven when you die?" Who in his right mind doesn't want to go to heaven? So a good number will say something like, "I *hope* I'm going to heaven when I die." Now say, "God wants you to have that assurance. All of us have sinned and come short of the glory of God, but God sent His Son to die on the cross for us so that we could have peace with God. When we repent and trust in Him, God will give us everlasting life. He writes our name in the Book of Life. Would you like to accept Jesus into your heart right now and have your name written in heaven? I could lead you in what's called a 'sinner's prayer' right now. Would you like to pray?" Many do.

You may ask a predictable, "What's wrong with that?"

Let me see if I can answer that question with an anecdote:

A blind sinner is unwittingly heading for a thousand-foot cliff. Modern evangelism draws alongside him and says, "Blind man, I am going to give you a wonderful gift that will give you peace." He then hands him a CD player and adjusts its earphones over his ears. The sightless man hears "Amazing Grace" being sung by a choir of ten thousand voices. His blind eyes widen with delight. He smiles and says, "What you said is true. This is truly wonderful. Thank you very much." He shakes the man's hand, turns up the volume on his newfound gift, and continues tapping his way toward the thousand-foot cliff.

Millions have been given assurance of salvation, but are strangers to biblical repentance.

What has modern evangelism done? It has failed to awaken the blind sinner to his true plight. Instead, it has given him *false* peace. Now he is not only still heading toward a horrible death, *but he is deaf toward any further verbal warning.* It has done an unspeakable disservice to the blind sinner.

Millions have been given assurance of salvation, but are strangers to biblical repentance. The Law has never awakened them. They have never been warned to turn from the cliffs of eternal destruction. Now, because of the techniques of contemporary evangelism, their ears are deaf to the true message of salvation.

A religious studies professor named Wade Clark Roof, in his book *Spiritual Marketplace: Baby Boomers and the Remaking of American Religion*, says that one-third of America's seventy-seven million Baby Boomers identify themselves as "born-again Christians." According to Roof, that means they've had a "highly personal spiritual experience that has changed their lives." Roof says only about half of those who call themselves "born again" today attend a conservative Protestant church. Twenty percent don't belong to *any* church at all, and a third of those who say they're "born again" believe in astrology and reincarnation.

There is even another hidden tragedy that has resulted from the efforts of modern evangelism. It doesn't take a rocket scientist to see that this nation has lost God's blessing. The American Cancer Society estimated that in just one year there were 1,382,400 new cancer cases. Add to that an onslaught of killer bees, massive hurricanes, devastating floods, earthquakes, droughts, tornadoes, etc. After years of evangelization by modern preachers, most Americans have a concept of God as a benevolent Father figure. Therefore, the terrible tragedies of "natural" disasters and deadly diseases that come our way are considered the mere rumblings of Mother Nature, El Niño, La Niña, global warming, global cooling—anything *but* the dealings of a holy God with a sinful nation. The thought that a God who is love would judge our nation with these catastrophes is unthinkable to many.

From there comes a tragic dilemma in which the Church finds herself: To go from preaching "God loves you" to "God is angry at the wicked every day" is too great a leap for her to take. Consequently, few preachers have the courage to say that America is under God's judgment, and those who do so are considered a little fanatical. Again, this is simply because just over one hundred years ago, modern evangelism forsook the scriptural *stepping stone*: the Law of God. Without it, the world cannot conceive that God would be angry at humanity. Remember, without the use of the Law, judgment is totally *unreasonable*. C. S. Lewis said, "When we merely say that we are bad, the 'wrath' of God seems a barbarous doctrine; as soon as we perceive our badness, it appears inevitable, a mere corollary from God's goodness." The Law helps us perceive our badness.

GOD IS NICE

A sincere young lady once heckled me as I expounded the Ten Commandments to a crowd of mainly unsaved people. She boldly called out, "Don't listen to this man! *God loves you.*" I stopped speaking and asked her if she cared about the salvation of those to whom I was speaking. She said she did, so I gently coaxed her up onto the soapbox and asked her to give her testimony. After she had (bravely) spoken for a few moments, I asked her where her hearers would go if they died without the Savior. She hesitatingly said, "Hell…" Then she began to weep and added, "…*but God is nice.*"

God is many things—holy, perfect, righteous, loving, good—but there is no biblical foundation for saying that He is "nice." The young lady was nice. She was charming. But to tell sinners that their Creator is "nice" will give the impression that He is "pleasant, sweet, delicate, and agreeable." If that was her image of God, no wonder she was offended by the biblical revelation of His nature. Sometime after that incident, another young lady publicly reproved me for preaching about future punishment. She called out "God loves you…just ask Jesus into your heart right now!" When I asked her where the crowd would go if they died without Jesus Christ she said, "They won't go to heaven." I asked where they would go. She said, "They won't go to be with God." Again I pressed her as to the specific location, and she said, "To a *not very nice* place." Her dilemma was that the mention of hell, without the Law to make it reasonable, made her God look like a tyrant and brought with it the scorn of the world.

Professor Douglas Groothuis of the evangelical Denver Seminary said, "Even some evangelicals, who generally take a more literal approach to biblical teachings, view hell as 'a blemish to be covered up by the cosmetic of divine love'" (*U.S. News & World Report*, January 31, 2000). They deliberately cover over any mention of the cliff toward which the blind man is headed. They don't want to alarm him.

No wonder the world has a misguided understanding of the nature of God. *The Washington Post* (January 9, 2000) put it this way:

> Over the years, Ed and Joanne Liverani have found many reasons to summon God. But now, at middle age, they've boiled it down to one essential: "Not to get clobbered by life."
>
> So sometime in the past ten years the Liveranis began to build their own church, salvaging bits of their old religion that they liked and chucking the rest. The first to go were an angry, vengeful God and hell—"That's just something they say to scare you," Ed said. They kept Jesus, "because Jesus is big on love."

At Camp Firefly, a yearly camp that my wife and I host for terminally ill children and their families, I went golfing with four of the fathers. On the first couple of holes, I made a few jokes and then used some "IQ test" tracts to break the ice for witnessing (see these unique tracts at www.livingwaters.com). All the dads failed the IQ tests, allowing me to remind them that sometimes our eyes can play tricks on us, keeping us from seeing the truth even when it is plainly in front of us. Then I asked who would like to take another intelligence test. "This time," I said, "it's about God." Two men came closer. Dan was one of them.

Dan had a very strong and friendly personality. He lived in the inner city with his wife and four children, and had had a very hard life. The first question on the test was, "Is there a God?" Dan said, "Yes." Second question: "Does God care about right and wrong?" Dan said, "No." The other men and I looked at Dan with a sense of wonder at how he could say such a ridiculous thing. I had never heard of anyone who believed that God didn't care about right and wrong, good and bad. When I asked the next question, "Is there a hell?" Dan didn't believe there was, because in his mind, if God didn't care about wrong then He certainly wouldn't create a place of punishment for wrongdoers.

It was obvious who I would be witnessing to on this golf outing. Before we teed off, I asked Dan how he would feel if someone took his wife into the field behind the golf course, abused her, slit her throat so she would bleed to death, and then stabbed her in the heart thirty times just to make sure she was dead. I asked him if he would care that someone did that to his wife. Of course, he did. He said, "I'd track him down and kill him myself." I then reasoned with him that if he, a mere man, cared about murder, how much more did God care about such a horrible act of violence. He didn't know how to answer other than to say, "God doesn't care about earthly things, only heavenly things." I felt that he was hiding something big, with an odd comment like that, but I didn't know what.

Then, following Jesus' example, and with the help of Dan's conscience and the Holy Spirit, I began to bring about the conviction of his personal sins. I did this by asking him if he considered himself to be a good person. He said, "Yes, I do." I asked him if he had kept the Ten

Commandments. He said he didn't think so, but that it didn't matter because he had plenty of relatives who went to church, and whose kids turned out far worse than his, concluding that his way was better. "Have you ever told a lie?" I asked him. He said he had. When I asked him what that made him, without hesitation he said, "A liar." I asked him if he'd ever stolen anything. Dan said, "Yes." I asked him what that made him. He said, "A thief." Then I told him that Jesus said, "Whoever looks at a woman to lust for her has already committed adultery with her in his heart." He easily admitted that he was guilty of looking at women with lust. Then I gently said, "Dan, by your own admission, you are a liar, a thief, and an adulterer at heart, and you have to face God on Judgment Day. And we've looked at only three of the Ten Commandments."

We went through some more of the Commandments, and by the next tee station, Dan had admitted that he was also an idolater and a blasphemer. I asked him, "If God judges you by the Ten Commandments on Judgment Day, will you be innocent or guilty?" He paused for a moment and said, "Guilty." I asked, "Do you think you'll go to heaven or hell?" He said, "I'll go to heaven because God is forgiving and He doesn't care about earthly things. All you need is a tiny bit of faith and He will forgive you of all that stuff." I said, "Dan, if you were a criminal, guilty of serious crimes, standing before a judge and you said, 'Judge, I know I'm guilty, but I have faith that you're a forgiving man, and that you'll just forget about what I did and let me go,' should that judge let you go?" He said no. We agreed that if a judge is a good judge, he cannot just overlook crime, but must see to it that justice is served and that criminals are punished. So

I asked, "Dan, do you think God is good?" He answered yes. I said, "If God is good, then by nature, He will not overlook your sins, but will do everything in His power to see that justice is served and that you are punished."

Dan said angrily, "Don't tell me that!" We picked up our golf balls, got into our cart, and drove to the next hole.

We had finished only five holes, and we weren't playing any more golf because we were so deep in conversation. The rest of the guys continued to play without us. Dan told me that his mother had always told him that he couldn't run away from God, that God would chase him down and would one day get him. Dan hated that. He was desperately trying to justify himself as a good person in his own eyes, believing that God didn't care about the sins of his past. I resumed the use of the Law. I told him that if he was honest, he knew that when God called him to give an account of his life on Judgment Day, he would be found guilty and receive the punishment he deserves. I shared with him what the Bible said about his fate: that all liars will have their part in the lake of fire, and that no fornicator, idolater, adulterer, thief, or blasphemer will inherit the kingdom of God. I explained that every time he sinned, he was storing up wrath for himself that will be revealed on the day of wrath, that he is an enemy of God because of his wicked works, and that "the wrath of God abides on him." I pointed out that if God gives him justice, he wouldn't be going to heaven, but would spend eternity in hell.

At this point, he had me locked in his stare, and I began to feel a great sense of pressure to stop the conversation. I knew I had to press on in our talk or the progress we had made would have been lost, and Dan would have been in a worse place spiritually than when we began. I had to continue reasoning with him until he stopped justifying himself and coming up with excuses for his guilt. It wasn't easy, but eventually his expression of anger toward me changed to a look of fear and panic. He was guilty, and he knew it. Dan wasn't defending himself anymore—just staring at me, looking like a man who had been found out and didn't know where to turn for escape. He eventually turned away from me and looked at the golf cart floor, as though he was coming to terms with the fact that he was guilty before God, and would one day be held accountable for his sins.

As he looked like his heart was sinking, I gently asked him if he could see his need for God's forgiveness. He said yes. Outside I was calm, but inside I was leaping with joy! Now that he knew his need for forgiveness, he could see his need for a Savior. Now was the time to tell him about Jesus. I said, "Although God is a God of justice, He is also a God of love and mercy, and He has made a way for you to be forgiven, Dan." He lifted his eyes and looked at me with curiosity. I said, "Dan, imagine that you're a criminal, guilty of serious crimes that have earned you a fine of five million dollars or a sentence of fifty years in prison. Without a dime to pay the court, you are being sent to prison for the rest of your life. Then suddenly, someone you don't even know steps forward and pays your fine for you. The judge examines the stranger's money and says, "Dan, this man has paid your fine in full. You are free to go." And then the stranger comes over to you and says, "I know you don't know me, but I sold my house and all my possessions, and emptied all my bank accounts to pay this fine for you. I did this because I love you." Dan was listening intently. Then I said, "Dan, that's what God did for you—He paid your fine. God became a man, Jesus Christ, and suffered and died on the cross to pay the price for your sin. You broke the Law and Jesus paid your fine. It's as simple as that. And you're free to go on the grounds that Someone has paid your fine. That's how much God loves you, Dan!"

I explained that he'd never be able to earn his way into heaven. He had lied, stolen, committed adultery, was guilty of idolatry and blasphemy, and had no excuse. But God will give him forgiveness as a gift if he will repent of his sins and place his faith in Jesus Christ alone to save him. We talked about what repentance meant. I told him the story of the Prodigal Son returning to seek the forgiveness of his father. The father, seeing him far off in the distance, actually *ran* to his son, picked him up and rejoiced, because his son was lost, but now is found, he was blind but now he sees! I told him that his mother was correct in saying that God had been chasing him all his life, but what he didn't understand was that He was chasing him in love, so that if Dan ever came to his senses and turned away from his sin to humbly seek God's forgiveness, he would find that He was very nearby. Dan sat still and quiet as I magnified the love, grace, and mercy of God in Jesus Christ.

I spoke to him about the urgency of his need to turn from sin and put his faith in Christ. I asked him if he thought it was possible that he could die that night. Dan's daughter had cancer—that was the reason he had come to Camp Firefly. He knew that tomorrows were never guaranteed, and understood that each day could be his last. I told him that because God's Word says, "Man is destined to die once, and after that to face judgment," nothing was more important than getting his heart right with God before he went to sleep that night. Dan nodded in agreement and said, "That's true."

We had reached the end of the golf course, each finishing with a score of 30! (We didn't mention to the guys at the clubhouse that we had played only the first five holes.) As the other guys in our group turned in their clubs, Dan and I were still talking in the parking lot. He sat down on the front of the golf cart and began to cry. He said, "I've been running from God all my life, trying to get away from Him. But I don't want to run anymore." He began to sob as he held his face in his hands. I put my arm around this big man and said, "Dan, do you need God to forgive you?" He said with a heavy voice, "Yes." I asked, "Do you want to turn away from all your sins and give your whole life to Jesus right now?" He said, "Yes, I do." In that moment, I was so overwhelmed with the Spirit's presence that I felt as though I was witnessing a miracle.

I told him to confess his sins to God—all of them. I told him that he needed to come totally clean before God and confess that he was a liar, a thief, and an adulterer. He must no longer hide his sins from God, but must forsake them all, and ask God to help him to turn to Him and to love and obey Jesus with all his heart. He began to pray, quietly confessing his sins to God. Then I prayed for him. I thanked God for chasing Dan and catching him that day on the golf course. I thanked Him for Dan's broken heart and willingness to repent of all his sins and trust in God's mercy. I asked the Lord to bless him, to protect him and his family, and to change him into a godly man. While I prayed, I could hear him quietly saying, "Yes, Father... in Jesus' name... in Jesus' name." We were two gathered in the name of Jesus, and I was sure that God had just soundly saved a man in the middle of a parking lot.

I asked him if he had a Bible; he did, and he was going to start reading it. We had become good friends and he had become a new creation. Later that day, I saw Dan sharing his story with another person from camp. He was tearing up again, sharing the story of the God who had chased him down on the golf course and caught him that day. I was later told that when Dan was asked how his golf game went, he said, "It was the best day of my life, and golf had nothing to do with it." —KC

A BURDEN FOR THE LOST

I n the blackness of Adullam's cave, David longed for a drink of the cool water of Bethlehem's well. Saul hounded him like a mad dog. Dare David risk being seen venturing outside the cave? Yet, his thirst would not subside. He remembered the hot days of his childhood, when his thirst drove him to draw fresh water from the deep well. The more he thought upon it, the more his desire grew, until he broke the silence and whispered, "Oh, that someone would give me a drink of the water from the well of Bethlehem, which is by the gate!" (2 Samuel 23:15).

The Scriptures then tell us:

> So the three mighty men broke through the camp of the Philistines, and drew water from the well of Bethlehem that was by the gate, and took it and brought it to David. Nevertheless he would not drink it, but poured it out to the Lord. And he said, 'Far be it from me, O Lord, that I should do this! Is this not the blood of the men who went in jeopardy of their lives?' Therefore he would not drink it. These things were done by the three mighty men (vv. 16,17).

The mighty three had a love for David that was more

167

than lip service, expressed by the fact that they risked their lives merely to get a drink of water for their beloved leader. Yet, David's reaction to their display of love was to pour the water out on the ground as a drink offering to the Lord.

Some may be tempted to say, "Surely, if those men went to such effort to get the water, at least David could have drunk it!" But we have here something far deeper than mere human gratitude. *David's conscience would not allow him to indulge in self-gratification.* He said, "This is the blood of the men who went in jeopardy of their lives!" *How could he drink it?* It was more than just a cup of water. It was an evident token, a symbol, proof of their love and devotion to him. The cost was too great. His only course of action was to give it to God, to pour that precious water out as a drink offering to the Lord.

> *The true convert holds the Cup of Salvation in his trembling hands. He has seen the cost of his redemption.*

ONE BIG GAP

My wife, Sue, was once awakened at 4:00 a.m. to the sound of the blaring television set. She immediately thought that one of our children couldn't sleep and was watching TV. However, it was so loud, she decided she would go downstairs and turn it down.

When she arrived in the den, she found that one of the family dogs had accidentally stood on the remote control and was watching the sports channel.

It fascinates us to see an animal imitate us with a wink or what seems to be a smile, or if it watches the sports channel. However, although evolution tries to link us to animals, there is one big gap. As humans, we know that we are "beings." We are aware of our destiny with death. We are aware of the existence of a Supreme Being. God has placed eternity in our hearts.

A non-Christian friend of mine found he had six months to live. His friends told him to spend the last six months doing a "brothel crawl." He wasn't interested. He found that he had something within his heart considerably stronger than his sex drive—it was the will to live. Deep within his heart he had a cry, "Oh, I don't want to die!" Eternity was in his heart. Its deep whisper was, "Oh, that one would give me a drink of water from the wells of salvation."

Before the beginning of time, God saw not only the cry of his heart, but the cry within every human heart. The Mighty Three, the Triune God, broke through the hosts of hell to draw water from the Well of Bethlehem. God was in Christ, reconciling the world to Himself. Now the offer to sinful humanity is: "Whoever drinks of the water that I shall give him will never thirst. But the water that I shall give him will become in him a fountain of water springing up into everlasting life" (John 4:14).

The true convert holds the Cup of Salvation in his trembling hands. He has seen the cost of his redemption. He sees that he was not redeemed with silver or gold, but with the precious blood of Christ. Like David, he cannot drink of that cup in a spirit of self-indulgence. Rather than drink in the pleasures and the comforts of the Christian life, his reasonable service is to present himself as a living sacrifice, holy and acceptable, and pour his life out as a drink offering to the Lord.

DELIGHTFUL HEART

I was killing time in a department store when an elderly man struck up a conversation with me. It wasn't long before the conversation swung around to the things of God. When I asked this man if he had a Christian background, his answer was interesting. He said, "Oh, I am a church-goer. I believe in God the Father; and the Son, *He's around too . . . somewhere.*" His reply was both humorous and tragic. This man went to church, obviously had faith in God, believed in the deity and the resurrection of Jesus Christ, *yet he was not saved.*

If you love God, your heart will go out to the millions who are in such a state. They are in the "valley of decision" (Joel 3:14). Valleys are often without direct light, and direct light is what sinners need. They don't understand the issues. They are so close to salvation; it is as near as their heart and mouth. Yet without repentance, they will perish. Such thoughts are grievous. If you are born of God's Spirit, you will find that something compels you to run to the lost, to reach out to the unsaved, because God gave you a new heart that delights to do His will.

Well-known author and pastor Oswald Chambers said, "So long as there is a human being who does not know Jesus Christ, I am his debtor to serve him until he does." Bible teacher C. F. W. Walthers said, "A believer is ready to serve everybody wherever he can. He cannot but profess the gospel before men, even though he foresees that he can reap nothing but ridicule and scorn for it; yes, he is ready also to give his life for the gospel."

One cannot help but see Peter's passion for the lost, so evidently portrayed for us in the Book of Acts. He put behind him the three denials of his Lord and stood before a multitude on the day of Pentecost. When a crowd gathered around the lame man who had been healed, he boldly preached the gospel to them. He testified before the very ones who had murdered the Savior, and he told them so.

He had a passion for his God and a passion for sinners.

What was the apostle Paul's greatest passion? This longing, this aspiration, this yearning, was simply for the salvation of the lost. His greatest passion was for evangelism, something made evident by his own words. In the introduction of his letter to the Romans, Paul said that he was in debt to the world. His evangelistic zeal was so great that he said he would give up his relationship with Jesus Christ if it would mean that his brethren would be saved. Look at these sobering words:

> I tell the truth in Christ, I am not lying, my conscience also bearing me witness in the Holy Spirit, that I have great sorrow and continual grief in my heart. For I could wish that I myself were accursed from Christ for my brethren, my countrymen according to the flesh (Romans 9:1–3).

I have looked at a number of Bible commentaries to see what they make of these verses. They have said that Paul could not be speaking of his own salvation. The reference is rather to Paul's willingness to be cut off from Israel. It's my understanding that the apostle was *already* cut off from Israel because of his faith in Jesus. If it was merely a reference to being cut off from his people, why did he say that he had *already* suffered the loss of all things? If they were but rubbish to him, why then does he have to back that up with (what seems like) oaths to make his point?

It is as though Paul was writing to hearers who would not be able to understand such love. How could evangelistic intensity weigh so heavy on a man that he was prepared to be cut off from any association with the Lord Jesus to see that desire fulfilled? Such a statement could not penetrate selfish minds without a thoughtful preparation. They would not believe him, so Paul testifies that in what he was about to say:

- He is telling the truth in Christ. The very One who was truth itself was Paul's witness that what he was about to say was true.

- His Holy Spirit–regenerated conscience bore witness that he spoke the truth. He had cultivated a conscience that was tender before God and man, and the "work of the Law" did not accuse him of lying. His words could not be dismissed as mere exaggeration, or even hyperbole.

Deep within the soul of this man of God lay a burden— a great sorrow, a continual grief. Horror of horrors—he was saved, but his brethren were not.

> "If sinners will be damned, at least let them leap to hell over our bodies. Let not one go there unwarned and unprayed for."

Perhaps you do think Paul was lying when he said that his concern for the lost meant more to him than his relationship with Jesus. Maybe he had no fear that all liars would have their part in the lake of fire. Perhaps he had no concern that in bearing false witness, he would transgress the Ninth Commandment, for which Ananias and Sapphira were swiftly struck dead in their crooked tracks. Of course, we can't be the judge as to whether or not Paul was telling the truth in Christ, that his conscience was bearing witness in the Holy Spirit, but there certainly is evidence of his evangelistic priority in his writings.

Moses said a similar thing when he asked that God would cut him out of the book of life, rather than judge Israel.

In light of these thoughts, I don't know how anyone can

call himself a Christian and not have concern for the lost. Charles Spurgeon said, "Have you no wish for others to be saved? Then you are not saved yourself. Be sure of that." He continued, "The saving of souls, if a man has once gained love to perishing sinners and his blessed Master, will be an all-absorbing passion to him. It will so carry him away, that he will almost forget himself in the saving of others. He will be like the brave fireman, who cares not for the scorch or the heat, so that he may rescue the poor creature on whom true humanity has set its heart. If sinners will be damned, at least let them leap to hell over our bodies. And if they will perish, let them perish with our arms about their knees, imploring them to stay. If hell must be filled, at least let it be filled in the teeth of our exertions, and let not one go there unwarned and unprayed for."

When an emergency vehicle drives through a city, the law demands that every other vehicle must pull over and stop. Why? *Because someone's life may be in jeopardy.* It is to be given great priority. That's how we should be when it comes to the eternal salvation of men and women. There is an extreme emergency. *Everything* else must come to a standstill, or we are in danger of transgressing the Moral Law, which demands, "You shall love your neighbor as yourself."

> I had no real concern for the salvation of others until I had the knowledge of the Law. When I understood God's holiness, and therefore His anger against sin, I began to see why Paul said, "Therefore, knowing the terror of the Lord, we persuade men" (2 Corinthians 5:11). —KC

Hell should be so real to us that its flames burn away apathy and motivate us to warn the lost. Do we see the unsaved as hell's future fuel? Do we understand that sinful humanity is the anvil of the justice of God? Have we ever been horrified or wept because we fear their fate? The depth of our evangelistic zeal will be in direct proportion to the love we have. If you are not concerned about your neighbor's salvation, then I am concerned for yours.

The evangelistic zeal described on the previous pages should characterize a normal, biblical Christian. However, according to the *Dallas Morning News* (June 11, 1994), sixty-eight percent of professing Christians outside of the "Bible Belt" don't see evangelism as being the number-one priority of the Church. Also in 1994, the Barna Research Group found that among American adults who said that they were "born again," seventy-five percent couldn't even define the Great Commission. A survey by *Christianity Today* (a major evangelistic magazine) found that only one percent of their readership said they had witnessed to someone "recently." That means ninety-nine percent of their readership were just "lukewarm" when it came to concern for the fate of the ungodly. According to *Zondervan Church Source*, ninety-seven percent of the Church has no involvement in any sort of evangelism. Only once in Scripture did Jesus give three parables in a row (Luke chapter 15). He did so to illustrate God's profound concern for the lost soul.

> *Hell should be so real to us that its flames burn away apathy and motivate us to warn the lost.*

How is it that so many who are within the Church can profess to love God, yet neglect or even *despise* evangelism? The answer is frightening.

THE RICH MAN

Some years ago, I read the story Jesus told of "Lazarus and the Rich Man," and interpreted it in a radically different slant than most. In fact, I have searched many commentaries and haven't found even one with the same interpretation. I submitted it to seven godly men. Six passed it as being biblically sound. The seventh wasn't too sure. I submit it to you for your consideration.

"There was a certain rich man who was clothed in purple and fine linen and fared sumptuously every day. But there was a certain beggar named Lazarus, full of sores, who was laid at his gate, desiring to be fed with the crumbs which fell from the rich man's table. Moreover the dogs came and licked his sores.

"So it was that the beggar died, and was carried by the angels to Abraham's bosom. The rich man also died and was buried.

"And being in torments in [hell], he lifted up his eyes and saw Abraham afar off, and Lazarus in his bosom. Then he cried and said, 'Father Abraham, have mercy on me, and send Lazarus that he may dip the tip of his finger in water and cool my tongue; for I am tormented in this flame.'

"But Abraham said, 'Son, remember that in your lifetime you received your good things, and likewise

Lazarus evil things; but now he is comforted and you are tormented. And besides all this, between us and you there is a great gulf fixed, so that those who want to pass from here to you cannot, nor can those from there pass to us.'

"Then he said, 'I beg you therefore, father, that you would send him to my father's house, for I have five brothers, that he may testify to them, lest they also come to this place of torment.'

"Abraham said to him, 'They have Moses and the prophets; let them hear them.' And he said, 'No, father Abraham; but if one goes to them from the dead, they will repent.' But he said to him, 'If they do not hear Moses and the prophets, neither will they be persuaded though one rise from the dead'" (Luke 16:19–31).

Is this a picture of the way of salvation? If it is, then it's totally inconsistent with every other biblical reference to deliverance from death. Those who would seek to justify good works as a means of entrance into heaven could find adequate evidence here. Let's look at the passage in the light of such a thought.

First, what was the rich man's sin? Obviously, it was failure to feed Lazarus. If that is the case, then he could have *earned* salvation. If a non-Christian wanted to earn his way into heaven, should he then give food to the homeless? How much food would merit eternal life? No, since salvation is "by grace [divine influence]...through faith...not of works" (Ephesians 2:8,9), the rich man's sin could not have been a mere failure to give Lazarus free food.

Perhaps his sin was the fact that he was rich. Then Abraham should have been damned, for he was rich. Was gluttony the rich man's sin? Not necessarily. According to *Vine's Expository Dictionary of New Testament Words*, "sumptuously" means "goodly."

Why the reference to his clothing? Was his apparel or the color of it abhorrent to God?

Second, what did Lazarus do to merit salvation? Did his suffering in this life appease the wrath of God, and gain him entrance into the next? If so, then let us seek suffering instead of the Savior. Let us inflict our bodies as did the prophets of Baal, or crawl up the steps of some cold cathedral until blood pours from festered wounds, then call for the dogs to lick them. If this is a picture of the way of salvation, then eternal justice can be perverted, God can be bribed, and the sacrifice of the wicked is not an abomination to the Lord.

The story therefore *must* have another meaning.

WHO IS THE RICH MAN?

Let us establish several principles of biblical interpretation that will help us unlock the meaning of the story of Lazarus and the rich man.

- Purple is the biblical color of royalty (Esther 8:15).

- Fine linen represents the righteousness of the saints (Revelation 19:8).

- The Church is referred to as the "royal priesthood" (1 Peter 2:9).

- The tabernacle (a type of the Church) was made of fine linen and purple (Exodus 26:1).

The rich man is a type of the *professing* Church, and the leper (which is what most Bible commentators agree he was) is a type of the sinner.

The foul sores of sin permeate his very being. He is as "an unclean thing." His righteousnesses are like filthy, leprous rags. Those who touch him are commanded to "hate even the garment defiled by the flesh" (Jude 23). Unclean spirits, like hungry dogs, feed off the wounds of his sin, waiting to consume him at death. He is laid at the gate of the Church—that rich, fat Laodicean Church...the "royal priesthood" of believers, clothed in fine linen and purple, faring sumptuously on the teachings of prayer, prophecy, providence, justification, sanctification, and purification. This Church enjoys an "abundant life" of men's camps, youth camps, marriage seminars, ladies meetings, worship, prayer, and praise; young people's meetings, Bible studies, audiotapes, videotapes, and CDs; it heaps to itself teachers, having "itching ears"—ears so scratched by feasting, so dulled by overconsumption, *that the muffled cries of Lazarus at the gate go unheeded!*

We have become like Israel when God spoke to them in their prosperity, but they said, "I will not hear" (Jeremiah 22:21). The sin of the Church isn't that it's rich, *but that it hasn't the compassion to throw even a few evangelistic crumbs to starving sinners at the gate.*

The rich man's thoughts are only for himself. He is filled with his own ways. We have built for ourselves big beautiful buildings, with cool clear acoustics and colorful carpets, where as cozy Christians we sit on padded pews, living in luxury while sinners sink into hell. We say that we are rich, but we are poor, blind, wretched, miserable, and naked. I thank God for comfortable pews and quality sound systems, *but not at the cost of neglecting the lost.* We have lavished luxury on the lifeboat, while people drown en masse around us.

I have watched vast multitudes crowd around ministries of "power," "healing," and "faith," and prayed that what I suspect is untrue. I have listened to the message that these men and women bring and hoped that I was mistaken in my thought that there was something radically wrong. I'm not bothered by what they say, *but by what is left unsaid.* There *is* healing in the atonement (who doesn't pray that God would heal a sick loved one?); we *need* to have faith in God's promises; and historically God does bless His people and lift them out of poverty, hunger, and suffering. *But why don't these ministers preach Christ crucified for the sins of the world?* They consistently leave the cross out of their message, other than to mention it as the means of purchasing healing and prosperity for God's people. Why is there no preaching against sin, and exalting God's righteousness?

I look at the vast seas of people before them and think that there must be many who don't know God's mercy in Christ, yet they are not warned to flee from the wrath to come. Judgment Day isn't mentioned, neither is hell, nor is there a call to repentance. I try to be gracious and excuse them by thinking that perhaps these are "teachers" within the Body of Christ, whose particular gifting is to exhort and encourage rather than to seek to save what is lost. However, the most gifted of teachers cannot be excused for not caring about the fate of the ungodly. The apostle Paul was the greatest of teachers, yet he pleaded for prayer that he would share the gospel with boldness as he "ought to speak." He said, "Woe is me if I do not preach the gospel!" (1 Corinthians 9:16). What are the ethical implications of a fire captain who is preoccupied with making sure that his firemen are well-dressed, while people he is supposed to be saving burn to death?

I pray that the following letter I received doesn't represent the throngs who are followers of these men and women. I tremble when I suspect that it does:

I don't think I've thanked you lately for waking me

out of my false conversion. Please don't let discouragement ever hinder you from continuing to preach "Hell's Best Kept Secret." I believe it's the perfect message to wake up anyone regardless of their denomination...*I never, ever thought the day would come that I would call myself an ex–"Word of Faith"er.* If Paul was a Hebrew of Hebrews, I was a faith guy of faith guys. A card-carrying, tape-listening-to, TV-preacher-watching, book-reading, seminar-attending, positive-confessing faith guy was I. And it was all a waste of time. I write this to show you that if one who was as extreme as myself can be snatched from such a slumber, I believe anyone with an ounce of self-honesty is a candidate for this wake-up call. Not that I am any more opposed to the errors of Word of Faith doctrine than those of others in contemporary Christendom, but it's what I'm most familiar with. Like any of them, its greatest error is that it's a broad way and a wide gate.

If the Prodigal Son had returned to his father *before* he realized that his desires were base, he may have come to him with a different attitude. Instead of seeing that his desires were for pig food and saying, "Father I have sinned ...make me like one of your hired servants," he may have said, "Father, I have run out of money." Rather than saying, "*Make* me," he would say, "*Give* me." Instead of wanting to serve his father, his father would become his servant. That is the category of many who sit in the midst of the Body of Christ. The Law has not been used to show them that their sinful desires are *exceedingly* sinful. God is merely a means to further their own ends.

ADMIRERS OF THE ADMIRAL
Few see how great a sin it is to neglect evangelism, because so few have any concern for the lost. Many within the

Church think we are here to worship the Lord, and evangelism is for the few who have that gift. Their call to worship is a higher calling.

There was once a respectable captain of a ship whose crew spoke highly of him. They said they esteemed him to a point where everyone knew of their professed love for him.

One day, however, the captain saw to his horror that an ocean liner had struck an iceberg and people were drowning in the freezing water ahead of his ship. He quickly directed his vessel to the area, stood on the bridge, and made an impassioned plea to his crew to throw out the life preservers. But instead of obeying his charge, the crew lifted their hands and said, "Praise the captain...praise you... we love you! You are worthy of our praise."

> *To lift our hands in adoration to God, yet refuse to reach out our hands in evangelism for God is empty hypocrisy.*

Can you see that the reality of their adoration *should have been seen by their obedience to his command?* Their "admiration" was nothing but empty words.

If we worship in spirit, we will also worship in truth. To lift our hands in adoration *to* God, yet refuse to reach out our hands in evangelism *for* God is nothing but empty hypocrisy. "You shall worship the Lord your God, *and Him only you shall serve*" (Matthew 4:10, emphasis added) is more than a mere satanic rebuke. If the average church made as much noise *about* God on Monday as it does *to* God on Sunday, we would have revival.

Yet, in his book *The Coming Revival*, Bill Bright reports that "only two percent of believers in America regularly share their faith in Christ with others" (NewLife Publications, p. 65).

Evangelist Bill Fay has spoken at more than 1,500 conferences and churches. At each meeting, he would ask how many had shared their faith in the previous year. Never once did he find a church where more than ten percent raised their hands. In December 1999, at a church of nearly 4,000 in Southern California, he found that only 12 had shared their faith in the previous year. Early in 2000, *The Gatekeeper*, a publication of a major denomination, revealed that ninety-seven percent of its membership will go to their graves without sharing their faith. Evangelism should be the life's breath of the Body of Christ. If the breath is not in the body, neither is the life.

This lack of concern for the lost may be because Christians haven't been taught the biblical priority of evangelism—even though it is so evident in Scripture. However, if we are aware of our debt to both Jew and Gentile, and yet refuse to hold out the Bread of Life, we prove to be the rich man of whom Jesus spoke.

> The problem is that we as Christians think that every person we speak to about the things of God is going to be contentious. We create our own monster. But that proves to be false...usually. You will find that most people appreciate that you have taken the time to care about them. Every now and then someone may be upset when you mention the things of God or hand out a tract. If that happens, quickly assure them that you didn't mean to offend them, look around for another horse, and get back into the saddle. —KC

I have always maintained that the very reason the Church exists on earth is to evangelize the world—to be a light in darkness, to preach the gospel to every creature. If we worship God, yet ignore His command to take the gospel to every creature, then our worship is in vain. It is to draw near to Him with our lips, but to have our hearts far from Him. I have often said that if you want to find the "evangelism" section in your local Christian bookstore, you had better take your magnifying glass. This is not the fault of the store, but is just an indication of where the modern church's priorities lie.

With this concern in mind, I wrote a book calling Christians back to evangelism, and sent the manuscript to an organization to review it. If they think the book has potential, they forward it to a publisher. This is what the reviewer said:

> I like the content of this manuscript very much. It contains a much-needed message for Christians about the Great Commission. Nevertheless, I see a serious problem when it comes to marketing this material. In order for a book to be marketed successfully in the bookstores, its identity must be clear. Where does this book go in the store? Is it a devotional book? Or a Bible study manual? Or is it an inspirational, "Christian living" book?

They rejected it on that basis. Despite it being a "much-needed message," they think the "serious problem" lies not in the Church itself but in the marketability of the message.

THE EVANGELICAL ENTERPRISE

One of America's most positively popular preachers once made a crystal clear statement that revealed his priorities. He said, "I don't think anything has been done in the name of Christ and under the banner of Christianity that has proven more destructive to human personality and hence counterproductive to the evangelism enterprise than the often crude, uncouth, and un-Christian strategy of attempting to make people aware of their lost and sinful condition."

What then does he consider to be the "evangelism enterprise" if it's not to warn sinners to flee from the wrath to come? It is clear what the problem is. Modern Christianity has degenerated into merely a means of self-improvement, self-esteem, and self-indulgence. It is self-centered rather than centered on and in the will of God. The same preacher reveals the cause of his error by saying, "The Ten Commandments were designed to put pride and dignity in your life." *That's not what the Bible teaches.* The Ten Commandments were given to do the exact opposite: to humble us. They show us that sin is "exceedingly sinful," and that we are in desperate need of God's mercy. The Bible tells us that the "Law brings about wrath" (Romans 4:15). It shows us the reality of God's wrath abiding on us. It is God's purpose for us to use the Commandments lawfully—to make people aware of their lost and sinful condition, "crude and uncouth" though it may seem to some.

In Luke 16:19, the rich man's problem was that he was idolatrous. His understanding of God was wrong. He lacked the knowledge of God and therefore didn't fear God, and because he didn't fear God, he didn't obey Him. He didn't love his neighbor as himself. Lazarus was starving at his gate, and he couldn't care less.

The irony of the story of the rich man was that he waited until he was in hell before he became concerned for others.

I have members of my own family who may never see the need to escape hell until they're already there. Then they will be concerned. If I am not concerned about their eternal destiny now, there's great reason for you to be concerned about mine. —KC

WHOSE COOKIES?

I f you witness regularly, you will know that many in contemporary America think they are good people. This is
the fruit of a nation that has forsaken God's Law. The Law
is "good," but when there is no knowledge of the Law,
"good" becomes subjective. This was the case with the rich
young ruler's question, "Good Teacher, what good thing
shall I do that I may have eternal life?" (Matthew 19:16).
Jesus reproved his misuse of the word "good." The young
man was one who used the word without knowledge of its
true meaning.

Sinners often say similar things. An athlete may say that
"the good Man upstairs" helped him win a race. Or they
seek to justify their sin by saying, "You're a good person;
tell me why the Bible says..." This is why I find it frustrat-
ing when I do a good deed for someone who doesn't know
that I am a Christian. If I help push a car, for example, I
don't want them to think, "I knew there were still good
people. That restores my faith in human nature." Often,
the more "good" people the world can find, the more they
will try to justify their own goodness and reject God's mercy.
Like the rich young ruler, they need to be enlightened as to
what *good* is. The way to do this is to follow the example of

Jesus and decimate the fig leaves of self-righteousness with the Ten Cannons of God's Law.

A famous Rogers and Hammerstein musical contained the words, "Somewhere in my childhood, I must have done something good." The young lady who was singing the song had fallen in love and was brimming with happiness. It was her way of saying that God was rewarding her with the blessing of true love because she merited it. While God does reward good and evil, her words exemplify the world's erroneous philosophy. Any good that comes our way doesn't solely come to us because *we* have done something good, but because God is good. Until we understand that "there is none who does good, no, not one," we will expect blessings because we think we are good and therefore deserve them. When life brings us suffering, we become angry at God because we think God owes us happiness.

An unregenerate world judges God as being the guilty party for the sufferings of humanity.

The Law not only gives us understanding of the grace of the cross, but of the grace of life itself—that He has not dealt with us according to our iniquities. The only thing God "owes" us is wrath.

A man in a London airport decided to purchase some English butter cookies. He opened the small tin, took one out then placed the tin at his feet. After he had waited for his flight for some time, a middle-aged woman smiled politely and sat next to him. To his astonishment, without a word of permission she reached down, took a cookie out of the tin, and ate it. He couldn't believe what this complete stranger had just done! Suspecting that it may be a local custom, he smiled at her and took one himself. A few minutes later, she took another one. He smiled awkwardly and took a second cookie himself. She then took a third. *Who did this woman think she was?* Then she took the very last cookie, looked at him, broke it in half and offered it to him. *The audacity of the woman!* Other words such as "brazen," "rude," "impudent," and "presumptuous" flashed through his mind.

As he was about to express his thoughts, he bent down and saw that his identical tin of cookies was still at his feet. In an instant, he realized that *he* had been the brazen, rude, impudent, and presumptuous person. *He had been eating the cookies of a complete stranger!* He also realized how her response to his actions had in truth been very gracious.

An unregenerate world judges God as being the guilty party for the sufferings of humanity. As far as they are concerned, He is unjust. But the Law of God gives us sudden light to our misconception. It shows us who is eating whose cookies. *We* are the ones who are in transgression. It dawns on us that we are *more* than brazenly impudent in our accusations. We are guilty criminals standing before an unspeakably holy and gracious Judge, accusing Him of transgression. In light of God's holiness, it is hard to understand why He continues to let a sinful humanity such as us even draw another breath.

FACIAL INJURIES

In March 1993, Sue and I were involved in a head-on collision. Fortunately, we sustained only minor head injuries. I was on my way back from the bathroom in the early hours of the morning when Sue got out of my side of the bed. For some reason she looked down for a second and we collided head-on, leaving us both with a fat lip. She presumed that I would see her in the dark, but I was coming from a bright light into a blackened room. I couldn't see a thing.

To presume that the unregenerate man already has the necessary light to be saved is to have a head-on collision with the many Scriptures asserting that there *is none* who understands (Psalm 53:2,3; Romans 3:11,12; 8:7). If we *adulterate* the Word of God by making the Law invalid in its lawful use of bringing light to the sinner, we will have *adulterous* converts. Their hearts will love the world and the things in the world. But as we "teach all nations" and, like the disciples, do not cease "teaching and preaching Jesus as the Christ," we will see sinners come to "know His will, and approve the things that are excellent, *being instructed out of the Law*" (Romans 2:18, emphasis added). "Instructed out of the Law" suggests more than a casual reference to the Ten Commandments. It means to rightly divide the Word of Truth, as a father at the head of a table would break up bread for his children.

Charles Spurgeon, in lecturing his students on evangelism, said, "Explain the Ten Commandments and obey the Divine injunction; 'Show my people their transgressions, and the house of Jacob their sins.' Open up the spirituality of the Law as our Lord did."

Pastor Jack Hayford wrote an article in which he spoke of many people coming to the Savior after he taught a series on the Ten Commandments. He said,

> As a pastor I've had to come to terms with a devastating fact: Through my teaching on God's grace, an alarming number of my flock have perceived that there is nothing to learn from the Commandments now that the Law, as a schoolmaster, has gotten them to Christ. Too many view their conversion as a graduation from accountability to the Law...which violates Jesus' own objectives.

He saw the consequences of an imbalance of Law and grace as being a "devastating fact." I would go further and say that what has resulted is utterly disastrous. This "alarming number" of people are not confined to his church. They think they have graduated from accountability to the Law and they therefore live their lives accordingly—in lawlessness. They have a mere "form of godliness." They are hearers and not doers; they listen to the sayings of Jesus, but don't do them.

SINNING CONVERTS

The direct result of the Church being confronted with biblical teaching on God's immutable Law would be that the "sinning convert" would no longer be consoled in his sins. Instead of dealing with the symptoms of the sinner's non-accountability lifestyle—his fornication, pornography, lack of discipline, lack of holiness, theft, wife beating, adultery, drunkenness, lying, hatred, rebellion, greed, etc.—the pastor would deal with the *cause*. He would say, "A good tree *cannot* bear bad fruit," and "no spring yields both salt water and fresh." He would gently inform his hearer, "It sounds as though you have had a spurious conversion and you need to repent of your lawless deeds and make Jesus Christ your Lord." Then, using the Law of God, he should show the "exceeding sinfulness" of sin and the unspeakable gift of the cross. This should awaken a false convert, put most Christian psychologists out of business, and cut "counseling" to a minimum.

A clear understanding of the reality of true and false conversion would give light to church leaders who are horrified at the state of what they see as the "Church." One respected leader said:

In survey after survey, researchers find that the life-styles of born-again Christians are virtually indistin-guishable from those of nonbelievers. The divorce rate among Christians is identical to that of nonbelievers. Christian teens are almost as sexually active as non-Christian teens. Pornography, materialism, gluttony, lust, covetousness, and even disbelief are commonplace in many of our churches.

Such teaching would also stop the insanity of modern evangelism's zeal without knowledge, by showing that the category of lukewarm "converts" doesn't exist. There is no division in the kingdom of God for those who are tepid.

> *Researchers find that the lifestyles of born-again Christians are virtually indistin-guishable from those of nonbelievers.*

We should be either hot and stimu-lating or cold and refreshing. Luke-warm "converts" are not part of the Body of Christ; they merely weigh heavy within the stomach of His Body until He vomits them out of His mouth on the Day of Judgment (Revelation 3:16). They didn't pass through the jagged-edged teeth of the Law of God. They remain hard and impenitent; they were never broken by the Law that they might be absorbed into the bloodstream of the Body of Christ, to become His hands, His feet, and His mouth. They never felt the heart-beat of God, so their hands didn't reach out in compassion to the lost, their feet were not shod with the preparation of the gospel of peace, and their mouths didn't preach the gos-pel to every creature.* This mass of converts is like the "backslider in heart," who is "filled with his own ways" rath-er than the ways of God. Their "Here I am Lord, *send him*," doesn't come from a fear of man, but from rebellion to the revealed will of the God they call Lord and Master.

Elisha told his servants to make some stew. However, "one went out into the field to gather herbs, and found a wild vine, and gathered from it a lapful of wild gourds, and came and sliced them into the pot of stew, though they did not know what they were." When the stew was being eaten, the guests cried out, "Man of God, there is death in the pot!" Elisha then put flour into the mixture, and "there was nothing harmful in the pot" (2 Kings 4:38–41).

The servants of the Lord have gone into the field of the world and brought back the wild vine of the modern gospel, which they added to the Church. Now there is death in the pot. What should give life-sustaining nourishment instead leads to death. As sinners are fed a gospel poisoned by modern evangelism, they are consuming a deadly mixture and becoming false converts.

The answer is to add flour. Flour is created by going through the process of brokenness; it has been ground to powder. The Law is the millstone that does that most necessary task.

THE WIDE GATE

In Matthew 7:13,14, Jesus said, "Enter by the narrow gate; for wide is the gate and broad is the way that leads to destruction, and there are many who go in by it. Because narrow is the gate and difficult is the way which leads to life, and there are few who find it."

Jesus warned that the way that leads to destruction was broad. But more than that, He said it had a "gate," and that "many" would "go in" that way. If the way of destruction is the way of the world, which is the usual interpretation, why did Jesus call it a "gate" that many would "enter"? Surely if that were the case, He would have said that the ungodly are *born* into the way of destruction. This thought is supported by the conjunction Jesus used to join verses 13 and 14. He said that the way of destruction is broad and many will enter into it *because* the way that leads to life is narrow. There are only two gates: if they don't go through the narrow, then they will end up going through the broad. He said the wide gate is entered *because* the other gate is narrow.

It seems rather that Jesus, in His usual consistency, is speaking of true and false conversions as He did in the Parable of the Sower, the Wise and Foolish Virgins, the Wheat and Tares, the Good and Bad Fish, the Goats and Sheep, and the Wise and Foolish House Builders. He again uses the word "many" here in describing them, as He did when speaking of the "workers of lawlessness" whom He never knew (Matthew 7:22,23).

Remember to what Jesus likened the kingdom of God? He said, "It is like a man going to a far country, who left his house and gave authority to his servants, and to each his work, and commanded the doorkeeper to watch" (Mark 13:34). The doorkeeper should keep the door. He should "watch," to allow in only those who should enter. Instead, we have forsaken our watch.

ACCEPTABLE FODDER

Again, the false convert is like the Prodigal Son *before* he understood that his appetites were base, that he had "sinned against heaven" and in his father's sight. Because modern evangelism fails to show him heaven's holy standard, he doesn't see that his sin is against God, so he thinks it is quite acceptable to desire "pig food." He returns to his father, but his heart is still with the harlots. He chooses to be with the people of God, but to secretly enjoy the pleasures of sin for a season. He also finds it easier to lie (white lies) than to speak the truth, easier to steal (white-collar crime) than to pay for something, easier to lust than to be holy, easier to live for himself than for others, easier to feed his mind on the things of the world rather than the things of God.

The professing convert's mind is on the things of the flesh *because he is still "bound by iniquity,"* as was Simon the sorcerer (Acts 8:23). Like Simon, he may believe, associate with the apostles, and see the miracles of God. He may pass through the waters of baptism and impress many with his subtle trickery, but those who understand the Parable of the Sower and its broad implications are not swayed. They see beyond his sleight-of-hand illusion into reality. They can see, to their horror, that the Church by preaching a Lawless gospel is ushering multitudes through hell's broad gate . . . a gate that is oiled smooth by modern evangelism.

> *The professing convert's mind is on the things of the flesh because he is still "bound by iniquity."*

Nehemiah chose two men to be in charge of gathering citizens for Jerusalem. Their names were Hanani, which means *gracious*, and Hananiah, which means *Jah (Jehovah) has favored*. Scripture tells us that Hananiah was faithful and that he feared God. This was what Nehemiah charged them: "Do not let the gates of Jerusalem be opened until the sun is hot" (Nehemiah 7:2,3). God has favored humanity with the gospel of grace. Those faithful servants who fear God will seek citizens for the New Jerusalem, and they will not open the gates until the sun is hot. They will let the heat of the Law do its most necessary work.

20

RAIDERS OF THE *CONTENTS* OF THE LOST ARK

As I sat in my car, I really did expect to receive a punch in the face. I had screened a series of television advertisements, warning of rock music that advocated violence and murder. One of the groups that stirred me to do so was called "The Dead Kennedys." Their songs include lyrics such as these:

> I kill children. I love to watch them die. I kill children, make their mommas cry. Crush them under my car, I love to hear them scream. Feed them poison candy, spoil their Halloween.

The advertisements had caused me to wonder if I would get my face rearranged by someone who didn't like what I had done. Now a gentleman in his forties, with a clenched fist and a determined look on his face, was making his way toward my car.

As he approached the open window of my vehicle, he looked me in the eye and asked, "Are you Ray Comfort?" I meekly said that I was. Then, without saying a word, he lifted his large clenched fist, thrust it toward me through the window, ... *and dropped $20 in my lap.* Then he walked off without a word.

It would seem that God delights in bringing victory out of what appear to be disastrous situations. Israel stood at the Red Sea, trapped, with no possible way of escape. Then God did the impossible. He brought victory out of what seemed to be a sure fist in the face. Daniel found himself in a pit of ferocious lions. Once again, God brought victory in the face of what appeared to be a devastating situation. Jesus of Nazareth had been crucified. The disciples had been scattered. It seemed that the body had been stolen. *How much darker could life become?* It was then that God revealed the brilliant light of the resurrection. He brought the ultimate victory out of the ultimate disaster.

CRIMINAL MORAL CODE

The story is told of a mother who rushed her 10-month-old baby, who had an acute case of diarrhea, to a hospital near her village in Bogota, Colombia. When she came to get her baby the next day, his eyes were bandaged and he was covered with splotches of blood. Horrified, she asked what was wrong with the boy, and was coldly dismissed by a doctor who told her that the child was dying.

In a panic, she raced her baby to another doctor who examined his wounds and said, "They've stolen his eyes!"

Her baby was the victim of "organ-napping," where eyes are removed and the corneas sold on the black market. In one sense the baby was fortunate—most victims are murdered.

In 1980, when the Ten Commandments were removed from the schools of the United States, the eyes of an entire generation were removed. The "Commandment is a lamp, and the Law a light" (Proverbs 6:23), and removal of the Law left a generation in the dark as to moral absolutes. We now live at a time when a breed of human beings can kill, steal, hate, dishonor their parents, and revile God without qualms of conscience.

In June 1993, six teenage gang members in northwest Houston raped and killed two girls ages 14 and 16. The leader of the gang, Peter Cantu (age 19), boasted how he and other members abducted the two young girls, raped and sodomized them before strangling them. According to their testimony, "It took a while for them to die." They kicked one girl in the mouth with a steel boot, knocking out three of her teeth, then strangled her with a belt until it broke. They strangled the other girl with a shoelace. Then they took turns stomping on their necks to make sure they died. These heinous crimes are all too common in our lawless society.

Today's generation doesn't just lack the moral values of its grandparents; it doesn't have any moral values. In previous years, there was a "moral" code even among criminals, an "honor among thieves"—that when they stole from someone, they didn't blast him with their gun as they left. This is not so nowadays. We are daily reminded that what one generation permits, the next embraces as normality. Years ago, a woman would hesitate to walk in front of a group of men for a concern that they would whistle at her and undress her with their eyes. Nowadays, her fear is that she will be viciously raped, sodomized, and murdered.

In light of the statistics we looked at in the beginning of this book, it would seem that the enemy has removed from the Body of Christ its ability to be salt and light in a dark and decaying world. Jesus warned that if salt lost its flavor, it would be good for nothing except to be trampled underfoot by men. This is why so many hold the Church in contempt. The world has trampled us underfoot, and is reaping terrible consequences.

We are living in times of gross darkness, but remember, this is not a "God-forsaken" world—it is a world that has forsaken God. He can, in His great sovereignty, open Satan's clenched fist and drop the riches of revival in the lap of the Church. Eric W. Hayden, in his book *Spurgeon on Revival*, wrote, "Almost every book dealing with spiritual awakening or a revival of history begins by describing the pre-revival situation in approximately the same words. For instance, you will read such words as these: 'The darkness before the dawn'; 'The sleep of midnight and gross darkness'; or 'dissolution and decay.' W. T. Stead, who was a child of the Welsh Revival of 1859, when writing of the later revival in the twentieth century, said of it: 'Note how invariably the revival is preceded by a period of corruption.'"

There is great hope for the masses of false converts who sit within the Church. It is a rich field of evangelistic endeavor. The fact that they are still there is a testimony to the fact that they remain open to the things of God. History shows us that virtually every major revival of the past has been birthed out of a great awakening of those who thought they were saved, but were not. I have seen this teaching awaken many false converts as to their true state. God has soundly saved them, and from there they have begun to be the witnesses they are commanded to be.

ENEMY ATTACK

Let me share with you some insightful words from Martin Luther. When speaking of using the Law as a schoolmaster to bring sinners to Christ, he said, "This now is the Christian teaching and preaching, which God be praised, we know and possess, and it is not necessary at present to develop it further, but only to offer the admonition that it be maintained in Christendom with all diligence. *For Satan has attacked it hard and strong from the beginning until present, and gladly would he completely extinguish it and tread it underfoot*" (emphasis added).

The enemy has duped the Church into believing that it is advancing by getting decisions for Christ. What has actually happened is that he has invaded our ranks and stripped the gospel of its power. The ark has been raided.

John Wesley said to those who forsook the Law in its capacity to prepare the heart for grace:

> *Virtually every major revival has been birthed out of a great awakening of those who thought they were saved, but were not.*

> O take knowledge what Satan hath gained over thee; and, for the time to come, never think or speak lightly of, much less dress up as a scarecrow, this blessed instrument of the grace of God. Yea, love and value it for the sake of Him from whom it came, and of Him to whom it leads. Let it be thy glory and joy, next to the cross of Christ. Declare its praise, and make it honorable before all men.

I know that his words are true. The enemy hates this teaching. I have many examples of the enemy's resistance, but one stands out in my mind. For years as I spoke on this subject, we tried to get a master audiotape of this teaching so we could share it with others. Each time we listened to the tape, we would find a mysterious "buzz" running through it, or a fifteen-second silence in the middle of an important illustration. However, in the late nineties, I spoke at a large church in Chicago that had a sophisticated sound system. They gave me a one-hour audio master with no flaws on the entire tape. That is, except for an eight-word sentence that had to be removed because it was cut in half when the sound man turned over the tape. That eight-word sentence that had to be deleted from a one-hour teaching was: "Satan doesn't want you to hear this teaching."

The devil is quite happy if the Church sings of the power of the presence of God. But remember that in the Old Testament, the ark of the covenant signified His presence. It wasn't the ark that God prized; it was what the ark *contained*. Have you ever wondered why it was that God manifested Himself in such a glorious way that the priests in the house of the Lord could not minister (1 Kings 8:10,11)? It happened when the priests brought in the ark of the covenant. Scripture tells what was in the ark:

> Nothing was in the ark except the two tablets of stone which Moses put there at Horeb (v. 9).

It seems God so esteems His Law that He could not withhold His glorious presence from the temple. The psalmist didn't say, "Oh, how I love Your *ark*!" Paul didn't say, "I delight in the *ark* of God." It was God's holy Law that they loved and revered. That Law was written with the finger of God. It was an expression of His character. We (as individuals and as the Church) are the "temple of the Lord," and when we give the Moral Law its rightful place, perhaps we will truly see that power of His presence—something that causes demons to tremble.

Satan hates this teaching for a number of other reasons.

1. It awakens the false convert to his true state.

2. It puts the fear of God in the heart of the Christian and therefore assists him to walk in holiness.

3. It gives him a reason to reach out to the lost. The issue isn't the happiness of sinners in this life, but their eternal welfare in the light of a wrath-filled Creator.

The following letter is typical of how the Law does its wonderful work:

> I am 53 years old. Have committed all sins. I was baptized and saved by God's grace...or so I thought. Have long sensed something wrong. Last week my wife picked up a free cassette tape ("Hell's Best Kept Secret") placed at the cash register of a local sandwich shop. I played the tape as soon as my wife gave it to me. Bingo! I immediately understood what was wrong. I had not been brought to salvation by the Law. At the same time [I realized] that evangelizing is what I am to do...I play HBKS daily and have lost count of how many times I have listened to it. God has my heart. I have absolute faith, a Bible, a box and lots of open air. Anxious for your reply.

The enemy has attacked the use of the Law in evangelism "hard and strong from the beginning until present." However, our great consolation is the fact that this is God's teaching, and I believe that it is His timing to bring it to light.

At the risk of sounding melodramatic, I would ask you to consider reading this book again, simply because experience has taught me that its truths will soon be snatched from your mind...unless you make a concerted effort to let them sink deep into the soil of your heart.

I have read and re-read this book many times. I have examined all the associated Scripture verses and determined that these principles are biblically rock solid. Nothing in all of our Christian life is more important than learning how to effectively bring lost souls to Christ. The Lord's passion is to reach sinners and save them from the fire; that's what He lived and died for. If we are following in the footsteps of Jesus, then it should also be our greatest desire—to seek and save the lost. —KC

It was A. W. Pink who said, "It is true that [many] are praying for worldwide revival. But it would be more timely, and more scriptural, for prayer to be made to the Lord of the Harvest, that He would raise up and thrust forth laborers who would fearlessly and faithfully preach those truths which are calculated to bring about a revival." The use of the Law in evangelism is the golden key to revival. It is heaven's answer to the prayers of those who yearn for the salvation of a hell-bound world. If we want to see revival in these last moments of time, we must take a firm hold of that key with unwavering conviction.

If we want to see revival, we must take a firm hold of that key with unwavering conviction.

Do you remember King David's experience with the ark (2 Samuel 6:3–8)? Instead of having the sons of Kohath carry it on poles as the Scriptures commanded, he put it on an ox cart. As the ark was brought into Israel, the ox stumbled and it began to rock. When Uzzah reached out his hand to steady it, God killed him. R. C. Sproul rightly said that Uzzah presumed his hand was cleaner than the dirt.

We have put the ark of the gospel on the ox cart of modern evangelism. Sincere though we may have been, we dare not presume that we can reach out our sinful hand and steady the things of God, and then carry on the way we have been going.

If we fear our Creator, we must discard our own ways, and then do all things according to the pattern given to us in Holy Scripture.

21

What About Grandma?

S omeone who had just heard the teaching expounded in this book, said, "I see what you are saying, and I agree with you. Let's say I'm on my way to witness to my elderly grandmother, who's not a Christian but thinks she is. Does this mean I'm going to have to say, 'Grandma, have you ever looked with lust?'"

Good question. The answer is a definite yes and no. Here's how you can say what you want to say without seeming disrespectful. First, gently swing to the subject by asking about her Christian background—when she started going to church, and so on. Then say, "You know what convinced me that I was a sinner? It was the Ten Commandments. I didn't realize that Jesus said, 'Whoever looks upon a woman with lust has committed adultery already with her in his heart.' I didn't know that God sees our thought life. Do you think that you have kept the Ten Commandments, Grandma? Would you consider yourself to be a good person?"

When she tells you that she's a good person, say, "Well, let's look at some more Commandments to see if we have kept them." Always bear in mind that you are not alone in your witness. You not only have the Holy Spirit to help, but you have Grandma's conscience working with you.

Earlier we looked at the story of the woman caught in the act of breaking the Law. She had violated the Seventh Commandment, and God's Law (and its professing representatives) demanded her death (John 8:1–11). Ignoring their accusations, Jesus bent down and wrote something in the sand that caused His hearers to come under conviction and leave. Have you ever wondered what it was that He wrote in the sand? Some think He wrote the sins of those standing around Him. If that were so, He would have no doubt needed a good-sized area of sand to write on.

We dare not point a finger at another when the ten condemning fingers of a holy Creator are pointed at us.

There is another way to convince people that they have sinned against God, and it doesn't require much writing. I suspect that when Jesus stooped down, He wrote the Ten Commandments. After all, what else does God write with His finger? (See Exodus 31:18.) The work of the Law was written on the hearts of His hearers, and they left one by one as their conscience did its accusatory duty, boldly verifying the truth of each Commandment. The Law strips us of our holier-than-thou self-righteousness. We dare not point a finger at another when the ten condemning fingers of a holy Creator are pointed at us.

It was the Law that brought the sinful woman to the feet of Jesus. It left her with no other option than to run from its wrath to the Savior. That's its function. The Law sends us to Jesus for mercy. But more than that, it is the wrath of the Law that makes us *appreciate* mercy.

We are also told that Jesus began to write as though He didn't hear them. There is no reasoning with the Law.

There is no insanity plea. It is written in stone. It grimly says, "The soul that sins, it shall die." The Law demands nothing but death. It doesn't hear a cry for mercy; it is cold and unmerciful. The ten great rocks of wrath call for justice and justice alone.

The first time God wrote His Law, it was engraved on hard stone. If it was the Law that Jesus wrote in the sand, it was symbolic that it can be erased only with a movement of God's mighty hand. That was what He did at the cross.

The Bible also tells us that the accusers came to "trap" Him. Arrogant and sinful man stands as the accuser of a sinless God. Do you know of a skeptic who mocks God and His Word? Does he accuse God of crimes against humanity? Does he think that God is responsible for famines and wars that are fought in His name? Then don't be afraid to shut the accuser up under the Law; stop his mouth (Romans 3:19). Turn the wrath of the Law on him. Show him that he, not God, is guilty of heinous crimes.

I have repeated myself a number of times in this book because I want these principles to become second nature to you. People sometimes ask what sort of results we achieve with this approach to evangelism. There are two answers to this question. First, we don't keep earthly documentation, simply because only God knows those who truly repent and trust Him.

Second, the criteria for judging this principle should not be how many "decisions" we get, but whether or not we are following in way of the Master. In earlier chapters we've looked at the biblical basis for using the Law in evangelism and seen how Jesus and the apostles used the Law to bring the knowledge of sin.

The testimonies throughout this book, as well as in the appendix, attest to the effectiveness of this method. However, using these principles does not, of course, guarantee the salvation of those to whom you witness. Let me share something very personal. To date, only one of my siblings or parents has become a Christian. My father made a number of professions of faith over the years, but there was never any fruit to confirm that he was genuinely saved. In July 2002, he had a heart attack, fell, and broke his hip. He was rushed to the hospital and it was found that his heart had only 15 percent of its capacity. As this happened 7,000 miles away (in New Zealand), I asked a Christian friend to visit him. He spent twenty minutes talking with my father, and then prayed with him for several minutes. I called the hospital and asked Dad if he was happy about that. He whispered, "Very happy." During this time, my brother, sister, and mother (none of whom are Christians) kept saying that there was a tremendous peace about him. Four pastors then visited him, and each assured me that it was evident that my father was genuinely saved. He died two weeks later, after some horrible suffering. There were many tears shed, but I thank God that He is faithful to His promises, and I'm looking forward to seeing my father again.

It has been thirty years since my conversion and I have diligently prayed for the salvation of my siblings and parents every day. They listen to me preach. They gladly take my books and tapes. They are not anti-Christian; they are just apathetic when it comes to their eternal salvation. *Yet I teach Christians how to share their faith effectively.* People draw on my "expertise" almost daily—and to my grief, *most of my own beloved family members are not saved.* This keeps me genuinely humbled, and shows me that what I share is not a "sure-fire method" to get people into God's kingdom. If it were, my entire family would be saved. It is instead *biblical* evangelism, and that means that no man can come to

What About Grandma?

the Son unless the Father draws him. It shows me that we can faithfully preach the Law, but it is a dead, dry, and dusty letter if not accompanied by the life of the Spirit.

THE MEASURING ROD

I'm sure you are equally concerned about the eternal salvation of *your* loved ones. In light of that, here's a thought-provoking question: How deep is your love? Here's the way to measure it. You are concerned about your immediate family's salvation, but what about your other relatives? How about your immediate neighbors? What about strangers? Are you concerned for the salvation of people you don't know? How about your enemies? Are you deeply worried about the salvation of people who have crossed you? Do you love your enemies enough to be troubled by the fact that they will go to hell forever if they die in their sins? If you have measured up to all of the above, congratulations —you are a normal biblical Christian, who has been commanded to love your enemies and to love your neighbor as much as you love yourself.

Here's one way to demonstrate the depth of your love. Do you say "hello" to strangers? It may not come naturally to you, but for the sake of the gospel, I would like you to try this experiment. The next time you are leaving a restaurant, or anywhere where someone is standing—maybe at a counter waiting to pay for something—study the person's facial expression for a moment. It will probably look a little grumpy. We don't like to admit it, but each of us does look a little grumpy while we are waiting for something; the burdens of the day tend to find expression through our face. Here now is the experiment. Forget about your fears, and with a warm and enthusiastic tone in your voice, say, "Hello." Then watch the person's expression change from grumpy to happy. They will almost certainly smile.

If by chance the person doesn't respond, you have lost nothing (you will just feel slightly silly). However, if there is a smile, there's your opportunity for the gospel. Reach into your pocket, and say (as if you had just thought of it), "Oh...did you get one of these?" (I do this with our tract "101 of the World's Funniest One-Liners."[10] With this tract, instead of being seen as a religious nut who is trying to ram religion down the throat of a complete stranger, I am seen as someone who is trying to brighten up the person's day.)

Here is something else that I have found to be very effective. One way you can gain instant credibility with young people, particularly teenagers, is to approach a group of two or three and ask, "Did you guys see this?" Then show them our pink and blue "Curved Illusion" tracts. That will get their attention. For credibility, have about ten one-dollar bills in your pocket, and ask (while holding the bills in your hand), "What's the capital of England?" When someone responds, "London," give him or her a dollar bill. If they don't know, ask for the capital of France, or the capital of your state. After two simple questions (and after giving another dollar bill) say, "Which of you folks think that you are a good person?" Usually someone will say, "I'm a good person!" Then ask, "Do you want to go for $20? I will ask you three questions. If you prove to be a good person, I will give you $20. Do you want to give it a try?" If one is interested in trying, ask the person's name and say, "Okay, John. I'm going to give you three questions to see if you are a good person. Here goes. Have you ever told a lie?"

Most people will say that they have. If John says that he hasn't, press him with, "Have you never told a fib, a white lie, or a half truth?" When he says that he has, ask what that makes him. Most will say, "Liar," while others may say, "Not a good person." If John doesn't want to call himself a liar, ask him what you would be called if you lied. That usually gets the person to admit that someone who has lied is called a liar. Once he has admitted that he is a liar, ask him if he has ever stolen something. If he says he hasn't, smile as you tell him that you don't believe him because he has just admitted that he is a liar. Then say, "Come on, be honest. Have you ever stolen anything . . . in your whole life . . . *even if it's small?*" When he says yes, ask what that makes him. He will more than likely say, "A thief."

Third question: "Jesus said, 'Whoever looks upon a woman to lust after her has already committed adultery with her in his heart.' Have you ever looked at a woman with lust?"[11] Males usually laugh when they say that they have, so soberly say, "John, by your own admission, you are a lying, thieving, adulterer-at-heart, and you have to face God on Judgment Day. If God judges you by the Ten Commandments on the Day of Judgment, do you think you would be innocent or guilty?" If he says, "Guilty," ask him if he would go to heaven or

> *You don't have to convince a sinner of the reality of Judgment Day. That is the work of the Holy Spirit.*

hell. If he responds, "Hell," ask if that concerns him. If he says, "Heaven," ask why. Then follow it with these verses (paraphrased): "All liars will have their part in the Lake of Fire" (Revelation 21:8). This verse may sound harsh, but quote it anyway. It's God's Word and it is quick and powerful. Also quote 1 Corinthians 6:9,10: "Do not be deceived. Neither fornicators, nor idolaters, nor adulterers, nor homosexuals, nor sodomites, nor thieves, nor covetous, nor drunkards, . . . will inherit the kingdom of God." This covers the First, Second, Seventh, Eighth, and Tenth Commandments. It also covers the Fifth. Someone who proves to be a lying thief has dishonored his parents' name. All you are wanting to do at this point is to awaken the person to the standard of God's Law and to their desperate state before the Judge of the universe.

Show genuine concern for their plight. Try to ensure that all of your hearers (other teenagers) are listening and let them know that they too have to face God. Say, "I don't want you to go to hell. You don't want to go to hell, and God doesn't want you to go to hell. Do you know what He did so that you wouldn't have to go there?" Then take them to the cross of Calvary, stressing their urgent need to repent, and inform them that they may not be here tomorrow.

One night in July 2002, I spoke with two young men —Kevin, 16, and Adam, 12—at our camp. My wife, Chelsea, spoke with them for an hour about the gospel, then she came outside and asked me to give them my testimony because Kevin's questions were so similar to my own as a teenager.

We three talked for two and a half hours. Kevin and Adam were so sure of themselves, so knowledgeable about religion, life, justice, etc. They had every question you could think of, and they were good and smart questions. I started by being a good listener and kept my mouth shut and ears open. I commended them on their questions and praised them for being real thinkers. Kevin had good intuition about truth. He said, "Why doesn't God just put something within us so that we will know what is true?" I told him about his conscience ("conscience" means "with knowledge") and his own spirit that will testify with God's Spirit that Jesus' words are true. I shelved other questions until later (about the Bible, evolution, etc.), but they never came up again.

I asked Kevin if he considered himself to be a good

person. He said yes. We went through most of the Ten Commandments and the consequences of sin according to God's Word. I used many analogies: raping and murdering his mom deserves judgment, the sheep standing on green grass looks clean until it snows, etc. Kevin and Adam threw in some divertive questions, but I tried my best to stay on course for the next half hour. Adam eventually got cold and went inside. Kevin and I sat and talked for another forty-five minutes. I repeatedly talked about his guilt and the consequences of sin in hell until I felt he understood. He said, "God is angry?" I told him that He was—"God is angry with the wicked everyday." When I felt that Kevin's mouth was shut up under the Law and he knew he was guilty, I moved on to the cross and God's mercy (giving the analogy of the guilty criminal whose fine has been paid).

Adam came back and listened to me talk to Kevin. I gave them my testimony and explained how I felt different after I had asked God to forgive and change me. Adam said, "It sounds like you felt almost like you were *born* again." I could hardly believe the words he chose to use. I couldn't have asked for a more beautiful confirmation and encouragement from the Lord—he was getting it! We then talked about why Jesus is the only way to be saved (the parachute given by the captain, Jewish sacrifices being a picture of Jesus' sacrifice). We talked about the difference between believing in Jesus and being born again. We talked about the horrible offense of rejecting God's Son when He is available to all people everywhere (I gave him the parable of vineyard owner, Jesus' words, etc.). I stressed the importance of the blood of Christ, the resurrection, and that good works will never work. We talked about a good tree producing good fruit, not fruit producing a good tree.

Kevin said things like, "I never understood why Jesus died on the cross until tonight." "So Jesus is our parachute!" Then he said, "You can't understand God until you understand why Jesus died on the cross."

Kevin asked if I ever sin. I explained the difference between running into sin and falling into sin. I also used the analogy of crocodile-infested waters to describe my desire to honor my Father's wishes.

Adam then said, "I'm getting a tingly feeling all over my body right now." He started to show signs of tenderness of heart. Kevin said he did too and that he felt that way whenever he is around someone he knows God is with. Adam said (with tears in his eyes), "This is a big night for me. I want to go write in my journal about this whole experience. This is a turning point for me, even if I am so young."

I told them the whole gospel, went over the Law and the cross again, and they both seemed to understand why Jesus is the only way to heaven. It made sense and was no longer offensive to them. I asked Kevin if he thought he could die tonight. He said yes, and we talked about the importance of getting his heart right with God. I told him that if he died in his sins, he was an enemy of God—that God's wrath was upon him and that he would perish under His judgment. He must turn from his sin once and for all, and put his faith in Jesus Christ alone to save him. I turned and applied it all to Adam also. I asked if I could pray for them both. They said yes. I prayed, and then asked them if anything I said offended them. They shook their heads no. I told them my motivation was that I want them to accept God's offer of love and forgiveness and escape the wrath to come.

They mentioned how Kevin had almost not come there that night and how thankful they were to be having this talk with me. I told them it is because God loves them and wants them to know the truth. When I shared about the Ethiopian eunuch to whom God sent a messenger, Adam said, "Just like you being here right now!" I also reminded them not to let this night pass, but to mark it their minds and hearts and let it be a new beginning, a new start, a new direction in their lives. I hugged them both and told them I loved them. They said goodnight, and went into their rooms; I sat down and prayed for their salvation.

Two days later Adam told me he'd been up all night thinking about what we had discussed. So had his brother. Then he said, "I want to reject all my sin and put my faith in God." He told me he wanted to be born again. I sat next to him and watched as he humbly confessed his sins to God and put his faith in Christ. Almost immediately, he told me that he really loved his family and wanted to share the gospel with them as soon as possible. He had acquired the fire. —KC

YOUR ROLE IN WITNESSING

Take great confidence that you don't have to convince a sinner of the reality of Judgment Day. That is the work of the Holy Spirit. John 16:8 says that the Holy Spirit will convict the world of sin, righteousness, and judgment. The mind of the unsaved cannot understand the judgment of God: "The wicked in his proud countenance does not seek God; God is in none of his thoughts... *Your judgments are far above, out of his sight*" (Psalm 10:4,5, emphasis added). The word used for "convict" in John 16:8 also means "to convince." Only the Holy Spirit can *convict* a sinner about his sin and *convince* him of judgment. We can't do that. All we can do is plant the seed of truth. When the sinner repents and trusts the Savior, it is then that the Holy Spirit dwells within him and seals him (John 14:17; Ephesians 1:13).

Neither is it our job to convince someone of the deity of Jesus. When Peter identified Jesus as the Son of God, He said, "Blessed are you, Simon Bar-Jonah, for flesh and blood has not revealed it to you, but My Father who is in heaven" (Matthew 16:17). It is God who reveals that great truth, so let Him do that task.

Forsaking the use of the Law in evangelism has made many in the Church think that apologetics are our great weapon in the battle for the salvation of the world. One could make a convincing case for that thought in this "age of enlightenment," when issues such as evolution and atheism have made these times unique in history. However, arguments come from the sinner's *intellect*. The ungodly mind is like a brick wall; it has been built to keep God out. It is at *enmity* with Him. It refuses to bow to the Law of God— "Because the carnal mind is enmity against God; for it is not subject to the law of God, nor indeed can be" (Romans 8:7). The human mind lays up arguments against God, so if you stay in that area you can expect a vicious battle. It is the mind that the Bible sites as the place of hostility—"And you, who once were alienated and *enemies in your mind* by wicked works, yet now He has reconciled" (Colossians 1:21, emphasis added). This wall of antagonism is hard and immovable, so make a habit of going around it. Learn to speak directly to the conscience (this is good news—it means we can be effective in our Christian witness without having to learn how to pronounce *Australopithecus afarensis*, or define the fossil record). When you address the conscience, these things become non-issues. It is that part of human nature that isn't an enemy of God. The conscience is God's ally. It doesn't speak against the Law of God; it speaks for it. It is the work of the Law written in their heart, "bearing witness" (Romans 2:15). It *testifies* for God. It is the trustworthy witness who points out the guilty party in the courtroom. Its mouth presents evidence of the Law's transgression. It is because of what it does that we should make room for it to speak as quickly as possible. If we want to win our case, we must bring out our star witness and put it on the stand to give it voice. We want to stop the mouth of the criminal, and that's what the lawful use of the Law does (see Romans 3:19).* It condemns the guilty and drives him to give up his defense, so that he will be forced to look solely to the judge for mercy.

> * Please don't skim over this point. It is so important it should be written across the sky. If you understand this biblical principle, it will revolutionize the way you witness. —KC

How wonderful it is, when talking with someone about the things of God, not to be thrown into panic when the person responds, "I'm a Roman Catholic." Before I understood the use of the Law I would think, "Horrors! Now I'm going to have to deal with transubstantiation, Mariology, papal infallibility, the mass, etc." Not so now. I simply say, "Would you consider yourself to be a good person?" I do the same with a Protestant. I do the same with a Moslem, an intellectual, an evolutionist, an atheist, etc. It is simply a matter of moving from the intellect to the conscience. (See the principles from this book in action in the movie *Left Behind II: Tribulation Force*, available through our web site.) Amazing as it sounds, although many Catholics have heard much about Jesus, the cross, sin, and salvation, most have never heard the true gospel. Our mandate is to preach the gospel to every creature (Mark 16:15), and it is the *gospel* that is the "power of God to salvation" (Romans 1:16). Once the Law is manifest, the usual rational arguments that so often cloud the issue become irrelevant.

Kirk shared the teaching on the use of the Law one morning at a large church in Ohio. A few days later we received an e-mail that shows the power of the Law to prepare the heart for the gospel:

> I just heard you speak this morning. I'm a Catholic—have been all my life. I can't even begin to tell you how much your message affected me. I've been quite speechless all day long, and I'm rarely quiet. It's been a good quiet because I am so humbled all of a sudden. I want to "take the ball and run with it," as you put it. However, I'm confused. You see, I've never been hit that hard in any Catholic service I've ever attended. How do you minister to Catholics? I can tell you that most of them don't want to hear anything unless it's from a priest. I could be wrong and hope that I am...but I'm full of questions on what to do next. Everyone needs to hear this message. My life has been changed since this morning. I can't thank you enough. I'm going to end here and start reading the book I purchased this morning! Thanks again and God bless you!

As mentioned earlier, we are to reason with a sinner using the Law. Never underestimate the power of reasoning about the reality of hell. Learn how to give extreme scenarios that stretch him into a moral dilemma. Say, "Imagine if someone raped your mother or sister, then strangled her to death. Do you think God should punish him?" If the person is reasonable, he will say, "Yes, of course. That makes sense." Then ask, "Do you think He should punish thieves?" Then follow with liars, etc. Tell him that God is perfect, holy, just, and righteous; that He will punish all sin, right down to every idle word, and that His "prison" is a place called "hell."

Always take him back to his personal sins. Remember to speak to his conscience—"You know right from wrong. God gave you a conscience," etc. Some people teach of a temporary hell (purgatory), or of "annihilation" (that the soul ceases to exist after death). The Bible, however, speaks of conscious, *eternal* punishment. If he thinks that is harsh, tell him that it is. If we think *eternal* punishment is horrific, what should we do about it? Shake our fists at God? When such foolish thoughts enter our minds, we must go to the foot of the cross and meditate on the great love God had for us—that He was in Christ reconciling the world to Himself. Then, we must turn any horror into concern, and plead with sinners to flee from the wrath to come.

C. S. Lewis seemed to sum up the terrors of hell when he said, "There is no doctrine which I would more willingly remove from Christianity than the doctrine of hell, if it lay in my power. But it has the full support of Scripture and, especially, of our Lord's own words; it has always been held by the Christian Church, and it has the support of reason."

That's why the Law is so wonderful. It gives hell rationality, and thereby gives access to a heart that was once closed. I found this to be the case just after the September 11, 2001, terrorist attack on New York. It's not every day that you see, live on television, 3,000 people go to their deaths in a matter of seconds. The experience left the whole world realizing not only their vulnerability, but also their own mortality.

A UNIQUE WITNESSING OPPORTUNITY

It was in that climate that I found myself speaking to hundreds of unsaved university students. I have often said that one good session of open-air preaching can reach more people in 30 minutes than the average church reaches in one year. There are a few drawbacks, though. It's difficult to get, and then hold, a crowd. Often hecklers create confusion. However, I think I may have found something that can reach more people in 30 minutes than many good open-air preaching sessions.

In August 2001, I called a large university in my home city (Christchurch, New Zealand) and spoke to the president of the Students' Association. I said that I would be visiting in October and would give any atheist an honorarium of $100 to speak for 25 minutes on "Why There Is No God." It would be a "debate," but without arguing. I would go first for 25 minutes, simply presenting my case for God's existence, and then my opponent would present his case and get $100 for his time.

He said it would be interesting, but doubted if many would show up as it was in the middle of exams. I said that I would like to try it anyway. A short time later I was informed that a resident professor of philosophy had agreed to the debate.

Here is the student president's promo letter:

> As exams are now with us, many students will be praying for a miracle. But is anybody listening? UCSA is proud to present the title fight to decide the heavyweight theory of the world.
>
> In the dark corner, hailing from UC's Philosophy Department and weighing in on the side of atheism—Dr. Paul Studtman.
>
> In the corner bathed in an ambient glow, the author

of *How to Make an Atheist Backslide*, and weighing in on the side of God Almighty—Ray Comfort.

At stake is a genuine offer from Ray Comfort of $US250,000 for anybody who can provide scientific evidence for the theory of evolution. For that sort of money Turi Hollis, the university chaplain, has been digging around in his 'not for public disclosure' files.

This meeting will not be broadcast on any network and is exclusive to: Shelley Common Room (upstairs at UCSA) at 1 p.m., Wednesday, Oct. 24.

I arrived in the hall on that date at 12:40 p.m. and found about a dozen people. At 12:45 p.m. there were about 100. At 1:00 p.m. the room was packed with hundreds of students on the floor, crammed into the doorways, and even packed down the halls. No doubt they wanted to see a Christian get eaten alive by a professor of philosophy.

I spoke for 25 minutes. The outline for God's existence was: 1) the evidence of creation; 2) the evidence of the Bible; and 3) the evidence of the conscience. When it came to the evidence of the conscience, I explained that if someone wasn't a Christian, his conscience was deadened, and I was going to resurrect it by going through the Ten Commandments. I explained that it wasn't going to be a pleasant experience—it was like looking into the mirror first thing in the morning (not a pretty sight)—but that it was most necessary to present my case, so I asked them to be patient with me. That gave me license to go through each of the Ten Commandments, then into Judgment Day, the cross, faith, and repentance.

The professor then shared his thoughts. His words were so big and his sentences so long that it was easy to forget the subject on which he began the sentence. Frankly, it was hard to stay awake. Then he had to leave after he finished speaking—which left me with hundreds of unsaved students asking questions such as "Who made God?" (one of my favorites).

During the presentation, I explained that evolution was unscientific and that there was no proof for the theory. I then told them to go to www.livingwaters.com and collect Dr. Kent Hovind's $250,000 offer—if they could "provide any scientific evidence for evolution." During the question time a student said, "I would like to know if anyone *does* have scientific evidence for evolution." There was a deafening silence as everyone waited for someone to say there was evidence. No one said a thing, so we went on to the next question.

> "The cross should be raised at the center of the marketplace as well as on the steeple of the church."

One older man (perhaps a professor) sarcastically asked if I believed in aliens. I told him that I did, and that California was having a problem with them coming across the border from Mexico. Everyone laughed, and he sat down.

I thanked them for listening. They gave a rousing applause. Every one of the 250 tracts I brought were taken from the table. Most of them were our skeptics' mouth-stopping tract, "Science Confirms the Bible." The professor was pleased with his $100, and I was ecstatic.

This is something that anyone can do. It is much easier than open-air preaching. There are no hecklers, the crowd is already there...and no one will beat you up. This is an unprecedented opportunity. Don't let fear stop you.

Remember, you don't have to debate or even have a question-and-answer time—just pray, present your evidence, and make tracts available. Make sure you speak first so that you won't be tempted to answer your opponent's objections and get distracted from your mandate. That mandate is simply to present the gospel—which is "the power of God to salvation."

Let me close with a quote by George MacLeod of Scotland:

> I simply argue that the cross should be raised at the center of the marketplace as well as on the steeple of the church. I am recovering the claim that Jesus was not crucified in a cathedral between two candles, but on a cross between two thieves; on the town's garbage heap; at a crossroad, so cosmopolitan they had to write His title in Hebrew and Latin and Greek...at the kind of a place where cynics talk smut, and thieves curse, and soldiers gamble. Because that is where He died. And that is what He died for. And that is what He died about. That is where church-men ought to be and what church-men ought to be about.

Thank you for being open-minded and allowing me to share my heart with you. May God continue to bless you and grant you your heart's deepest desires, as you delight yourself in Him.

APPENDIX

When we follow in the way of the Master and use the Law to bring the knowledge of sin, it is sure to impact our witness. The following testimonies relate how individuals have been affected by learning this biblical principle.

I was one of those who thought that preaching "Christ crucified" alone [without the use of the Law] was the way to go as far as winning souls was concerned. Boy, was I wrong. I have told people about Jesus many times in my life and have led many in the "sinner's prayer," and then afterwards I would ask them, "If you died right now, where would you go?" Many of them would answer, "Heaven," and I would say, "That's right." What I did was help to create false converts who are now convinced that there is no way they could go to hell. I have really messed up. I never again want to be that type of hindrance to the Body of Christ, or to those who are lost and going to hell. You have truly helped to change my whole understanding of salvation and soul winning.

Whew! This is a very "meaty" book! It is not something to read lightly. After reading the quote about Kirk's own reaction to the truths of this book, I can certainly echo his sentiment! While the concept of personal repentance is not new to me or my witness, this book is a powerful affirmation of the urgency for including the Law in the gospel presentation, so that it can do the work that it was created to do. I wonder if we (the modern evangelical church, in general) do not omit the Law in our witness out of a misplaced sense of compassion, i.e., that we can spare the sinner the anguish of personally interacting with the Law as a condemned person. What that compassion overlooks is the fact that this is exactly what we need to do. I think so far the most powerful analogy in this book for the works of the Law and grace is the needle (which must be sharp and strong) and the thread, which is silken and follows the needle in after it has opened the way.

I just have to tell you how thankful I am for your ministry. It is causing a revolution in my life. Yesterday I watched the new video on your site, "How To Break the Ice." Today I visited a nearby skateboard park and had a great conversation with four skaters. I went through the Law with them, and talked about judgment, etc. Even though we had fun, it was easy to see conviction come over them. I couldn't believe my ears when one of them suddenly folded his hands and, as though his friends weren't there, he began to pray for forgiveness! Wow. I've had 13 years of *no* fruit at all, and I have evangelized a lot in street meetings, door-to-door, etc. To see teens have true conviction and pray from their hearts because they know they are sinners...well, this is not a normal experience for me, to say the least. It's like heaven has come to earth (and it has).

I've always had a hard time witnessing to people— knowing how to approach someone and what to say. Kirk's story about witnessing at the golf course brought a new light to my heart. Everyone knows the Ten Commandments, but I would never have thought to use them to witness to anybody. That story was so touching and uplifting. To know that you can use a tool like the Ten Commandments to lead someone to the Lord is just amazing. I've been browsing through this web site and I can't believe all the things I have read so far. I am an assistant youth leader. I'm just starting out but this site has taught me so much more about how to witness, among other things, that I really feel will be beneficial to bring to my youth.

In all honesty I have been hiding in the safety zone of the church for the last five years. I have always believed that my big destiny was to teach, and I have been perfectly comfortable doing that until I heard "Hell's Best Kept Secret." *Congratulations*—you and the Lord have blown me right out of my comfort zone! If I don't do something with this fire inside me it will burn out... I want to bring people into the kingdom of God.

I have started to use your method of going through the Ten Commandments one by one, and showing how we have all broken each one and are under the death penalty. Last night a lady came under the conviction of the Holy Spirit and gave her life to the Lord. She said that she had never seen the depth of her sin like that before—and she was weeping that she had grieved God. She said that she could not wait but needed to commit her life there and then. Praise God for His truth and for people like you who have redirected us back to the core of the gospel message. I have never been afraid of speaking on sin and hell before, but this is first time that I have actually used the Ten Commandments in such a way.

My wife and I both listened to the tape "Hell's Best Kept Secret." We feel you are right on with your teaching. I have been reading *Revival's Golden Key*...This is one of those defining moments for me...Great book. It makes it all very clear and inexcusable. How can we not preach the Law and its payment for sin? I'll give this book to all my youth pastor friends and anyone else who can read! Thanks for your insight and boldness to stand in the face of 60 years of modern evangelism and its diluted means.

I was so surprised to see Kirk Cameron at a funeral. When he got up to speak and started talking about the Ten Commandments, I thought, "Oh, he's just going to be superficial; how sad." Then he started being direct, and he made me think about my life. It seemed like everyone in the room disappeared and I was totally focused on his message. I was blessed by it and I can't get it off my mind.

Mr. Cameron, I heard you speak in Knoxville, and I have never had the gospel preached to me in the way you did. You made a great impact on my life which I will always remember. Thank you for your dedication and your love for the Master. Because of your message I have rededicated my life to Christ, and both my wife and I are going to live our lives as we should, and live for Him and praise His name. Hopefully I can take a little of what you said and spread it to someone else. I am only a vessel and I want the Lord to use me in any way possible. Again, I just wanted to thank you for your obedience to what God has called you to. Yesterday I had the privilege of leading three folks to the Lord. I talked to two sisters (in their early twenties), and I took them through the Law first and then grace. Their father overheard and came in, and all three bowed their hearts to the Master! I have lead more people to the Lord in the last 40 days than I did in all of last year. Knowing what to teach and how to present it gives me confidence. I'm not trying to beg people to take Jesus—no, after they see how utterly sinful they really are, they want Him, really want Him.

For a long time I allowed myself to fall into the "soft" gospel approach—witnessing without preaching the reason why sinners will go to hell. There are so many subtle reasons to "soften the blow" to make it "seeker-sensitive," but it cheats those I witness to. Your tape has changed my perspective and my outlook on sin as more serious, which drives a greater burden for witnessing.

I wanted to tell Kirk Cameron that I was so impressed with his lesson last night. I was at the First Baptist Church of Concord in Knoxville, Tennessee, and was just amazed. I have been a Christian for ten years and have always struggled with witnessing. I have always had a desire to witness, but have usually failed. I love this approach and I will be learning as much about it as I can so that I can share the good news and reach people.

About two months ago I gave your book to a friend of mine who is a pastor. Since he has read the book I have seen a great change in him. I believe your book is crucial for many reasons. It all goes back to Truth vs. "feel good" gospel. And your book has not only caused me and my pastor friend to scream "bloody murder" over the false gospel that is being presented time and time again, but it has also caused us to check the status quo on all things. It has awakened us to challenge the way our church has operated

—seeking "success" instead of excellence, preaching "feel good" messages instead of God's Word and Truth.

Just listened to Ray Comfort's message—*it is terrific!* I confessed my sins of omission in not preaching the Law, which at one time I did, but got away from doing. This is revival in my heart! *Thank you, Lord Jesus!*

I am 42 years old and have shared my belief in Christ for almost 20 years, but I have never seen anything as powerful as the teaching I have received from you guys. I have watched young men weep when confronted with their sin against God, and have watched old men literally fall to their knees when they see themselves the way God sees them. (It is incredible—I have never witnessed anything so awesome in my life.) I have seen confessed witches' hearts change. I have seen hundreds of young men and women in Juvenile Detention cry and squirm under the weight of the Law. I feel that God has given me a new direction in life because of your willingness to obey. Thank you. Praise God for what you are doing, and may His blessing continually be upon you.

This letter isn't intended to be some "pour your heart out, gushy, tear jerker, crying in the coffee" letter (I do that with my Lord). It is just to say that your book, *Revival's Golden Key*, woke me up. I realized while reading that I was taking advantage of the grace Christ had given me. I saw myself before a holy, gracious God, and was found lacking.

I just got through reading *Revival's Golden Key*. It has deeply challenged everything I have ever thought about witnessing to nonbelievers. I have also listened to your tape

"Hell's Best Kept Secret" several times, and it has been a blessing to me. I'll be the first to admit that I have tried to bring sinners to salvation with the "God-shaped hole in your heart" style of evangelism. It's interesting that I tried to witness that way, because I knew (my conscious bearing witness) that I myself was a wicked, nasty sinner who was deserving of eternal flames. Yet I would preach "Jesus loves you." I guess I was just a product of modern evangelism. Anyway, I'm grateful for what the Lord has done in your life and how He is using you to reach sinners. In my witnessing now, I make sure to use the Ten Commandments, knowing that the sinner cannot "know sin, but by the Law." However, I'm still not where I need to be in witnessing. I ask that you would pray for boldness for me in witnessing. I have no problem talking to people, it's just that initial contact that I struggle with.

I have been camp pastor at four youth camps so far this summer and am halfway through. I must say that your tape "Hell's Best Kept Secret" and your book *Revival's Golden Key* have had a huge impact on my ministry. The messages that I have preached and my dramas are flooded with God's Law, and I have seen so much more brokenness in the decisions this summer than ever before. A church in Louisiana had sent me your tracts for years, and I had gotten your book about a springboard to powerful preaching many years ago, but this has had a *much* bigger impact on my life. I wanted to say thanks for sharing this.

I must admit, I went to the church with great excitement to get to see Kirk Cameron. I was a big fan. Not that I don't like you now, but it's for such a different reason. I was amazed, blown away by what you said. I soaked it all up and am still on fire because of it. I told everyone in the weeks leading up to your appearance that I was going to get to see you, maybe get an autograph. Once I heard you I forgot why I had come in the first place. I even got up to the table to talk to you, and instead of asking for an autograph, I had to tell you that I learned from you. I wasn't interested in you as a star, but as a brother in Christ—let me tell you, that amazes me. I totally got what you were saying! I had a chance to witness to my cousin last week, and I really messed it up and didn't even get a single point out. I was so disappointed in myself, but I am going to study my notes that I took and pray about it, and I will go back to her. I am so excited about this web site and about the Academy. I plan on learning everything I can and really doing my job as a Christian and spreading the good news. I am so excited—I told everyone I saw about it today. I can't stop thinking and talking about it. I want to thank you for showing me a different way. It just makes so much sense!

A friend recently directed me to your web site to listen to "Hell's Best Kept Secret." I was so excited after hearing the message that I downloaded all of your messages available for that purpose and am in the process of listening to them. They have stirred within me the fire to share my faith with others like never before! I accepted Christ 30 years ago, but my passion for evangelism has waxed and waned over the years... until now. Some of your examples in "How to have passion for souls" were especially striking, and caused me to think about the lost in a new way. This morning, I went running with a group of men. We run three times a week for fellowship and exercise. At 38, I am the youngest of the group. One of our runners is a 50ish surgeon of Jewish descent who does not know Christ, and in fact does not know Judaism either. He shared that his 80-year-old father has a tumor in his kidney that may be cancer. This brilliant, intense surgeon looked me straight in the eyes and said, "What happens to your soul when you die?" I immediately thought of just answering his question and seeing where the conversation went from there, but then I stared back into his eyes for several seconds and saw pain, fear, and uncertainty—things rarely seen in men of his intellect and position until they are face to face with death. This stirred within my heart such compassion for him that I explained to him why we are all sinners, using the methods you shared in your sermons regarding the Ten Commandments. We went around the circle and each man admitted that he had, at some time in his life, broken every commandment. (These are prominent men in the community who are disciples of Christ.) Then I explained to him that the penalty for sin is to spend eternity in hell—eternal torment and separation from God. Then I explained that Jesus shed His blood to pay the price for our sins, and that the only way to avoid the penalty of death was to confess our sins to God and ask Jesus to be the Lord and Savior of our lives. This surgeon did not make a commitment to Christ this morning, but I was able to share the gospel of Christ with him out of compassion, on terms he understood using the Law, which he knew from his Jewish heritage, and various examples from your messages.

I have just been so blessed the last three months to have you disciple me with all of your teachings. I just got back from a youth camp in Louisiana, and I want you to know that I used the "Have you ever told a lie?" scenario with five youth, and all broke down in contrition and repented and put their faith in Jesus.

I just witnessed to my two favorite nephews for two and a half hours. It was a beautiful work of the Lord. They started out proud and full of knowledge, and they ended up humbled, quiet, and thanking me for helping them see for the first time why Jesus died on the cross (they have grown up Catholic). They had tons of initial objections to Christianity and Scripture, but all melted away in the heat of the Law against the conscience and then the story of God on the cross saving them. *Yeehaaa!!* I am pumped, and so grateful to God for this opportunity. They are so precious to me. I've been waiting for this conversation for many years! Another example of how nothing but the Law would have worked here. Can you tell I'm excited?

I have been engrossed in your tape series "Hells Best Kept Secret" and your book *Revival's Golden Key*. I feed on these constantly. I have pastored for over eight years and these materials are sure answering a lot of questions for me. I am from the Word of Faith camp, so I was attentive to the letter you published in the book. I have certainly seen the abuses of the faith message and have done it myself. But instead of throwing it all away (we must live by faith), I am just reexamining my heart and will use the faith concepts for souls instead of always focusing on my needs, etc. This message definitely needs to invade the Faith camp as well as all other camps.

I want to thank you for doing God's will because I am now reaping fruit from what I heard you preach. I was searching and I knew something was missing. I knew it was personal evangelism, but I didn't know how to share or even what to share (although I knew it wasn't "Jesus loves you and has a wonderful plan for your life"). I was impressed by what I had read. Your teachings allowed the Holy Spirit to set me on fire! I have reaped more fruit in the last month than in probably my whole life.

On March 1, 2002, after listening to "Hell's Best Kept Secret" for the fourth time, an anointed light bulb went off in my head. I jumped up and ran around the house yelling, "I understand! I understand!" I ran up to my dad, gave him a hug and said, "Dad, I understand!" His response was, "What?" Until that day, I had never heard of Judgment Day, never used the Law, and didn't even fear God! I had what you would call "an idolatrous idea of God." During the last few months, God has been showing me how to fear Him and the horror of what I've been saved from. Every night, and every morning, I feel the length of eternity on my heart.

Your ministry has touched me and my husband so deeply. Never have we burned with passion for God's Word and purposes as we do now after listening to your tape "Hell's Best Kept Secret."

I have attended church my entire life. I'm 28, a deacon and youth leader. I have known I am a sinner and accepted Christ as my Savior as a young child, but I always thought I was missing something and I just couldn't put my finger on it. Once I listened to "Hell's Best Kept Secret," I was blown away. Why hadn't I ever been taught like this before? I examined myself, and my salvation became so much more real. I felt so alive and free and full of joy that I just had to tell everyone I knew. I have been revived and want to seek and save that which is lost. I now hunger and thirst for righteousness and no longer care about the things of the world.

I guess I would say I am one of those "Word of Faithers"... My spiritual "walls" went up, but my curiosity won out and I began reading. I was almost immediately enthralled. That night I woke up at 3 a.m. thinking about the book. I got up and continued reading. It has consumed my thoughts for the past several days. I feel so convicted that I too have been deceived, slumbering—and still I feel that my heart is somewhat callous, as though I were in a state of shock. I am so grateful for this spiritual awakening. I wish I could give this book to all of my friends (Christian and not), our pastor, my family. Thank you, thank you, *thank you* for having the courage to speak the *truth* in love. I feel as though a great light has shone on me. Perhaps this message will be responsible for ushering in revival.

NOTES

1. See "Closing Words of Comfort" in *The Evidence Bible* (Gainesville, FL: Bridge-Logos).

2. Read the whole story in *Miracle in the Making* by Ray Comfort (Bridge-Logos Publishers).

3. Asking what Jesus would do is a good principle to live by—for a Christian who understands Scripture and has a tender conscience. Otherwise, this principle is open to abuse: "What would Jesus do? I'll tell you what He *wouldn't* do. He wouldn't condemn people because they want an abortion, or go around ramming religion down people's throats!" The principle becomes open-ended so that people can make up "another Jesus" to fit anything they would like to do. The better question is to ask, "What *did* Jesus do?" This confines us to the safe boundaries of holy Scripture.

4. I see nothing unbiblical about a call to the altar for prayer. However, I believe that it is a great mistake to use music to stir a response. Music plays to the emotions of the human heart. It can produce fear, peace, joy, tension, etc., and can easily bring us to tears. Think of it like this: A little child has broken something I told him not to touch. I soberly challenge him with, "I told you not to touch that. *Are you sorry for what you have done?* Before you say anything, let me put on some gentle music to help you make up your mind." That would stir his emotions, when instead I should be appealing to his will and conscience.

5. The audiotape version of "Hell's Best Kept Secret" can be heard free online at www.livingwaters.com.

6. For further teaching on how to use the Law to bring the knowledge of sin, see my books *Hell's Best Kept Secret* (Whitaker) and *How To Win Souls and Influence People* (Bridge-Logos).

7. We have an open-air preaching video called "In Season, Out of Season" (showing open-air preaching in Santa Monica, London, Paris, Amsterdam, New Zealand, and Tokyo) in which you can see Lazarus in action. See www.livingwaters.com or call 800-437-1893 for details.

8. The woman at the well is often cited to justify that we come to Jesus for happiness. However, to say that the "thirst" spoken of in John 4:13–15 is a thirst for happiness is mere conjecture. The *biblical* reason we come to the Savior is for *righteousness*, not happiness. The only way for this woman to drink of the living waters of eternal life, was to pass through the door of *righteousness*. Jesus said that those who hunger and thirst for *righteousness* are blessed (Matthew 5:6). He said that unless our *righteousness* exceeds that of the scribes and Pharisees, we wouldn't enter the kingdom of heaven. He told us to seek first the kingdom of God and His *righteousness*. This woman had transgressed the Seventh Commandment, and without the *righteousness* of Christ, she would perish. The Law makes us thirst after a righteousness that we have no desire for.

9. I give away money because it gets the attention of sinners. Jesus referred to money in His preaching (He borrowed a coin for a sermon illustration, and even had someone retrieve one from the mouth of a fish). If the lost don't love God, they will love money. Money is their source of joy. It is their security. When money speaks, they listen.

10. See www.livingwaters.com or call 800-437-1893.

11. I normally deal first with lying, stealing, and lust, because people can more easily acknowledge them as evident "sins." It seems that this is what Jesus did in Luke 18:20.

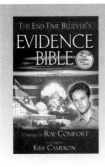

The End-Time Believer's
EVIDENCE BIBLE

"*The Evidence Bible* is specially designed to reinforce the faith of our times by offering hard evidence and scientific proof for the thinking mind."
—DR. D. JAMES KENNEDY

The Evidence Bible, based on more than two decades of research, has been commended by Josh McDowell, Franklin Graham, Dr. Woodrow Kroll, and many other Christian leaders.

- Learn how to show the absurdity of evolution.

- See from Scripture how to prove God's existence without the use of faith.

- Discover how to prove the authenticity of the Bible through prophecy.

- See how the Bible is full of eye-opening scientific and medical facts.

- Read fascinating quotes from Darwin, Einstein, Newton, and other well-known scientists.

- Read quotes about the Bible from presidents and famous people.

Discover how to answer questions such as: Where did Cain get his wife? Why is there suffering? Why are there "contradictions" in the Bible?... and much more!

The End-Time Believer's Evidence Bible (Bridge-Logos Publishers) is available at your local bookstore.

For a catalog of books, tracts, tapes, and videos by Ray Comfort, visit our web site at www.livingwaters.com, call 800-437-1893, or write to: Living Waters Publications, P. O. Box 1172, Bellflower, CA 90706.

THE WAY OF THE MASTER
Video Series

"The Way of the Master" video series is a condensation of the teaching presented in this book.

Tape 1 is a slightly edited version of "Hell's Best Kept Secret" by Ray Comfort, introduced by Kirk Cameron.

Tape 2 is titled "True and False Conversion," also introduced by Kirk, and *Tape 3* is titled "WDJD?" (What Did Jesus Do?). In it, Kirk and Ray walk you step-by-step through how to witness to atheists, the self-righteous, false converts, and "motor-mouth" talkers, and what to do when you can't answer a difficult question. You can see both of them witness to more than a dozen people. Also available on DVD.

To order, see www.livingwaters.com or
call 800-437-1893.

RAY COMFORT's ministry has been commended by Franklin Graham, Dr. D. James Kennedy, Josh McDowell, David Wilkerson, Bill Gothard, Dr. Jerry Falwell, Joni Eareckson Tada, George Barna, and many other Christian leaders. He has written for Billy Graham's *Decision* magazine and Bill Bright's *Worldwide Challenge*. He has preached in over 700 churches; his videos have been seen by more than 30,000 pastors; and millions of his gospel tracts are sold each year. His literature is used by the Moody Bible Institute, Leighton Ford Ministries, Campus Crusade for Christ, Institute in Basic Life Principles, and the Institute for Scientific & Biblical Research.

Ray is originally from New Zealand, where he preached "open air" over 3,000 times before moving to the United States. He has written more than 35 books, including *Hell's Best Kept Secret*, which has sold more than 100,000 copies. In 2002, Ray Comfort's *The Evidence Bible* was nominated as a finalist for the prestigious Gold Medallion Book Award. He lives with his wife, Sue, and their three grown children in Southern California.